Islāmic Integrated Narrative Therapy

This book explores the integration of narrative therapy within the framework of Islāmic psychotherapy, combining modern therapeutic practices with the rich cultural and spiritual heritage of Islām.

Narrative therapy, which emphasises the importance of personal stories in shaping an individual's identity and experiences, finds a natural complement in the Islāmic tradition, where narration has always played an important role. This integration provides a culturally sensitive therapeutic model that respects and utilises the client's faith and cultural background. The book details how narrative therapy principles align with Islāmic teachings, particularly the emphasis on introspection, personal responsibility, and the transformative power of stories found in the Qur'ân and hādith. It provides detailed guidelines and techniques for therapists to use narrative therapy with Muslim clients, including culturally relevant storytelling methods and exercises. These techniques are illustrated with real-life examples and case studies. In addition to practical techniques, the book addresses the ethical considerations involved in integrating narrative therapy with Islāmic psychotherapy along with emerging trends, ongoing research, and potential areas for further development.

This book offers an original contribution by developing a culturally and spiritually integrated model of narrative therapy tailored for Muslim clients. By aligning therapeutic techniques with Islāmic teachings, it provides mental health professionals with practical, faith-sensitive tools, making it especially valuable for therapists, counsellors, and scholars working within Muslim communities.

G. Hussein Rassool, PhD, is Professor of Islāmic Psychology at the Centre for Islāmic Studies & Civilisations, Charles Sturt University, Australia. He serves as Director of Studies at the Department of Islamic Psychology, Psychotherapy & Counselling, Al Balagh Academy. He is also Chair of Al Balagh Institute of Islamic Psychology Research and Director of Academic & Clinical Affairs at Sakina Way (Online Addiction Service), https://www.sakinaway.com. He is Director of Academic Affairs and Consultant, Yashfeen Psychiatry & Islamic Psychology, Bangladesh. He is also involved in mentorship and supervision at the Department of Islamic Psychology, Mind and Brain Hospital, India.

Focus Series on Islāmic Psychology and Psychotherapy
Series Editor: Professor Dr. G. Hussein Rassool, Professor
of Islāmic Psychology.

About the Series

In contemporary times, there is increasing focus on the need to adapt
approaches of psychology, counselling psychology and psychotherapy to
accommodate the integration of spirituality and psychology. With the increasing focus on the need to meet the wholistic needs of Muslims, there was a call
to adapt approaches to the understanding of behaviour and experiences from
an Islāmic epistemological and ontological worldview.

The aim of the Focus Series on Islāmic psychology and psychotherapy is
to introduce a range of educational, clinical and research interventions relat-
ing to Islāmic psychology and psychotherapy that are authentic, practical,
concise, and based on cutting-edge research. Each volume focuses on a particular aspect of Islāmic psychology and psychotherapy, its application with
a specific client group, a particular methodology or approach, or a critical
analysis of existing and emergent theoretical and historical ideas.

Each book in the Focus Series is written, in accessible language, with the
assumption that the readers have no prior knowledge of Islāmic psychology
and psychotherapy.

**Quranic Concepts in Islamic Psychology and Spirituality: Application in
the Modern World**
By Zuleyha Keskin

Ethical Foundations and Guidelines in Islāmic Psychology
By AbdulGafar O. Fahm

Working with Crisis and Trauma from an Islāmic Perspective
*By Zarina Hassem, Shireen Ismail, Nabeela Vad Walla,
Dr. G. Hussein Rassool*

Islāmically Integrated Psychotherapy and Domestic Abuse
By Khalida Haque

Islāmic Integrated Narrative Therapy
By G. Hussein Rassool

Islāmic Integrated Narrative Therapy

G. Hussein Rassool

R Routledge
Taylor & Francis Group

LONDON AND NEW YORK

First published 2026
by Routledge
4 Park Square, Milton Park, Abingdon, Oxon OX14 4RN

and by Routledge
605 Third Avenue, New York, NY 10158

Routledge is an imprint of the Taylor & Francis Group, an informa business

For Product Safety Concerns and Information please contact our EU representative GPSR@taylorandfrancis.com. Taylor & Francis Verlag GmbH, Kaufingerstraße 24, 80331 München, Germany.

Trademark notice: Product or corporate names may be trademarks or registered trademarks, and are used only for identification and explanation without intent to infringe.

British Library Cataloguing-in-Publication Data
A catalogue record for this book is available from the British Library

ISBN: 978-1-032-95452-3 (hbk)
ISBN: 978-1-032-95456-1 (pbk)
ISBN: 978-1-003-58499-5 (ebk)

DOI: 10.4324/9781003584995

Typeset in Times New Roman
by codeMantra

Dedicated to Asiyah Maryam bint Adam Ibn Hussein Ibn Hassim Ibn Sahaduth Ibn Rosool Ibn Olee Al Mauritiusy, Isra Oya, Idrees Khattab, Adam Ali Hussein, Reshad Hassan, Yasmin Soraya, BeeBee Mariam, Bibi Safian & Hassim, Dr Najmul Hussein and Mohammed Ali.

لَّقَدْ كَانَ فِى قَصَصِهِمْ عِبْرَةٌ لِّأُولِى ٱلْأَلْبَٰبِ ۗ

- *There are certainly in their stories a lesson for those of understanding.* (Yusuf (Joseph) 12:111, interpretation of the meaning)

"Indeed, in their stories, there is a lesson for men of understanding. It (the Qur'ân) is not a forged statement but a confirmation of the Allah's existing Books [the Taurat (Torah), the Injeel (Gospel) and other Scriptures of Allah] and a detailed explanation of everything and a guide and a Mercy for the people who believe." (Muhammad Taqiud-Din alHilali)

Contents

Figures

Tables

Focus series: background and context

Over the past four decades, there has been a noticeable revival of interest in Islāmic psychology and its practical applications across various domains, though largely within specialised circles. This renewed engagement has been accompanied by an expanding body of literature dedicated to Islāmic psychology and psychotherapy, reflecting a growing recognition of the need to address the holistic well-being of Muslims through approaches that are consistent with Islāmic values and worldviews. The *Focus Series* is a direct response to this emerging demand. These books are intentionally concise, practical, and grounded in evidence, designed to offer clear and accessible insights into Islāmic psychology and psychotherapy. Avoiding unnecessary complexity, the series aims to serve as a reliable resource for students, academics, clinicians, and the wider public seeking to engage with the field in a meaningful and informed way.

Aims of series

The *Focus Series* on Islāmic psychology and psychotherapy is dedicated to integrating Islāmic principles into the theory and practice of psychology, with a particular emphasis on educational, clinical, and research contexts. Its goal is to promote psychological well-being and personal development through insights rooted in the Islāmic tradition. By presenting authentic themes alongside contemporary research, the series strives to make Islāmic psychology and psychotherapy more accessible and relevant to educators, clinical psychologists, psychotherapists, and counsellors, ultimately contributing to the advancement of this evolving field.

Preface

In recent years, narrative therapy has gained prominence as a postmodern approach that helps individuals shape meaning and identity through the stories they tell. By re-examining and rewriting these narratives, clients can reshape their experiences and find new ways to navigate challenges. As psychotherapy continues to evolve, there is increasing awareness of the importance of cultural and religious sensitivity, particularly when working with diverse populations such as Muslims. Traditional Western approaches, rooted in secular, individualistic, and Eurocentric frameworks, often overlook the spiritual and communal values that are fundamental to cultures like Islām. For Muslim clients, effective therapy calls for an integrative approach that interlaces together psychological principles with Islāmic spirituality and theology. Culturally adapted methods like narrative therapy enhance outcomes by aligning with clients' beliefs, values, and worldview. Within an Islāmic framework, this means integrating Islāmic epistemology, spiritual practices, and culturally meaningful narratives into the therapeutic journey.

Narrative therapy aligns well with Islām's tradition of storytelling as a tool for teaching, healing, and transformation. The Qur'ān, hadīth, and historical narratives are filled with stories that offer profound moral, emotional, and psychological insight. Accounts of Prophets Yūsuf, Ayūb, and Mūsā (عليهم السلام) illustrate enduring lessons on trauma, patience, resilience, courage, and spiritual growth. Incorporating these narratives into therapy helps Muslim clients reframe their struggles not as random suffering but as divinely guided trials with purpose. This perspective fosters hope, meaning, and a deeper connection to Allāh throughout the healing process.

Islāmic Integrated Narrative Therapy, the central theme of this book, introduces a therapeutic model that blends narrative therapy with Islāmic teachings, offering a spiritually and culturally grounded framework tailored for Muslim clients. It equips therapists with practical tools, such as Qur'ānic storytelling, metaphors, and spiritual narratives, to support clients in re-authoring their life stories in ways that are both meaningful and transformative. Through detailed case studies and real-world applications, the book demonstrates how narrative techniques can effectively address various mental health challenges within an Islāmic context. It serves as a vital resource for Islāmic psychotherapists, mental health professionals, psychologists, and counsellors working with Muslim populations. Additionally, it provides valuable insight for students, scholars, and anyone interested in the integration of Islām and psychotherapy, offering strategies for faith-informed therapeutic practice.

Acknowledgements

All Praise is due to Allāh, and may the peace and blessings of Allāh be upon our Prophet Muhammad (ﷺ), his family, and his companions.

I would like to express my heartfelt gratitude to Grace McDonnell, Publisher at Routledge, for her invaluable guidance and insightful suggestions during the revision of this book's proposal. My sincere appreciation also goes to Alice Maher, Editor at Routledge Mental Health, for her continued professional support, which has been deeply valued. I am also thankful to the Editorial Assistants at Routledge, whose behind-the-scenes dedication and consistent assistance have played a significant role in bringing this project to completion.

I would like to acknowledge the support and encouragement of my colleagues at the Centre for Islāmic Studies & Civilisations, Charles Sturt University, Australia. I am especially grateful to Dr. Zuleyha Keskin, Associate Head of School, for her continued support and encouragement. My heartfelt thanks also go to the past and present students of the Islāmic Counselling and Psychology (Level 2), Addiction Counselling and Islāmic Psychology, Islāmic Marriage Counselling, and Mental Health, *Jinn* Possession and Islāmic Psychology courses at Al-Balagh Academy. Their dedication, curiosity, and engagement have provided me with valuable insights and deepened my understanding of Islāmic psychotherapy and counselling. I also extend my sincere appreciation to Dr. Md. Shariful Islam, Trustee and Board Member of Yashfeen Psychiatry & Islāmic Psychology, Bangladesh, for his unwavering commitment to advancing the field of Islāmic psychology and psychotherapy.

I am deeply grateful to my beloved parents, whose unwavering love, guidance, and emphasis on the value of education have profoundly shaped the person I am today. Their wisdom and encouragement continue to inspire me in every step of my journey. I am also sincerely humbled by and thankful for the enduring love and support of Mariam, Idrees Khattab Ibn Adam Ali Hussein Ibn Hussein Ibn Hassim Ibn Sahaduth Ibn Rosool Al Mauritiusy, Adam Ali Hussein, Reshad Hasan, Yasmin Soraya, Isra Oya, Asiyah Maryam, Nabila Akhrif, Fatima Ezzahra Bennaoui, Dr. Najmul Hussein, and Mohammed Ali. Each of them has been a source of strength, inspiration, and encouragement.

Their presence in my life is a true blessing, and I am forever indebted to them for their support and love.

I am sincerely grateful to my teachers, whose invaluable contributions have profoundly shaped my understanding of authentic Islām. Through their guidance, I have been able to walk the path of knowledge in accordance with the Creed of *Ahlus-Sunnah wa'l-Jamā'ah*. Their teachings have been instrumental in grounding this work in sound Islamic principles.

I humbly pray that Allāh forgives me and accepts this modest effort. May He make this book a source of benefit for all who engage with it, and a means of guidance for those seeking knowledge and understanding. Any clarity or benefit found in these pages is solely by the Grace of Allāh, and any errors are mine alone. I ask Allāh to pardon any unintentional shortcomings and to allow this work to serve a fruitful purpose for all those who find value in it.

مَّآ أَصَابَكَ مِنْ حَسَنَةٍ فَمِنَ ٱللَّهِ ۖ وَمَآ أَصَابَكَ مِن سَيِّئَةٍ فَمِن نَّفْسِكَ ۚ

- *Whatever of good befalls you, it is from Allāh; and whatever of ill befalls you, it is from yourself.* (An-Nisā' 4:79).

بِسْمِ اللَّهِ الرَّحْمَٰنِ الرَّحِيمِ

Praise be to Allāh, we seek His help and His forgiveness. We seek refuge with Allāh from the evil of our own souls and from our bad deeds. Whomsoever Allāh guides will never be led astray, and whomsoever Allāh leaves astray, no one can guide. I bear witness that there is no god but Allāh, and I bear witness that Muhammad is His slave and Messenger. (*Sunan al-Nasa'i: Kitaab al-Jumu'ah, Baab kayfiyyah al-khutbah*).

- *Fear Allāh as He should be feared and die not except in a state of Islām (as Muslims) with complete submission to Allāh.* (Ali-'Imran 3:102, interpretation of the meaning).[1]
- *O mankind! Be dutiful to your Lord, Who created you from a single person, and from him He created his wife, and from them both He created many men and women, and fear Allāh through Whom you demand your mutual (rights), and (do not cut the relations of) the wombs (kinship) Surely, Allāh is Ever an All-Watcher over you).* (Al-Nisā' 4:1, interpretation of the meaning).
- *you who believe! Keep your duty to Allāh and fear Him and speak (always) the truth).* (Al-Aĥzāb 33:70, interpretation of the meaning).
- *What comes to you of good is from Allāh, but what comes to you of evil, [O man], is from yourself.* (An-Nisā 4:79, interpretation of the meaning).

The essence of this book is based on the following notions:

- The fundamental of as a religion is based on the Oneness of God.
- The source of knowledge is based on the Qur'ān and *hādīth*. (*Ahl as-Sunnah wa 'l-Jamā'ah*)
- Empirical knowledge from sense perception is also a source of knowledge through the work of classical and contemporary Islāmic scholars and research.
- Islām takes a holistic approach to health: physical, psychological, social, emotional, and spiritual health cannot be separated.
- Muslims have an Islāmic or Qur'ânic worldview different from the Western-oriented worldview.

It is a sign of respect that Muslims would utter or repeat the words 'Peace and Blessing Be Upon Him' after hearing (or writing) the name of Prophet Muhammad (ﷺ).

Note

1 The translations of the meanings of the verses of the Qur'ān in this book have been taken, with some changes, from Saheeh International, The Qur'ān: Arabic Text with corresponding English meanings.

Section 1

Theoretical and conceptual model

1 Foundations of narrative therapy

Introduction

Narrative therapy is a postmodern, client-centred approach to psychotherapy developed by Michael White and David Epston in the late 20th century. It views identity as shaped by the stories individuals tell and share. Unlike traditional therapies that focus on diagnoses, narrative therapy adopts a non-pathologising stance, separating problems from the person. Through externalisation, clients can view their issues as distinct from their identity, allowing them to re-author their life stories with new meaning and direction. This approach highlights the power of language and narrative in shaping reality, acknowledging that experiences are influenced by personal and cultural contexts. Clients are encouraged to reconstruct their narratives based on their values, goals, and strengths. Maladaptive behaviours are seen as responses to external influences rather than fixed traits, fostering self-compassion and change. Narrative therapy can be used with individuals, couples, and families to enhance psychological well-being, emotional expression, resilience, and coping. It empowers clients to replace self-defeating stories with strength-based ones, promoting growth and healing. According to White & Epston (2009), Wallis et al. (2011), and Harms (2007), the core aim is to transform negative narratives into empowering ones. This chapter will explore the theoretical foundations, therapeutic process, client–therapist relationship, and key techniques used in narrative therapy.

Concept of narrative therapy

White and Epston (2009) define narrative approaches as centring individuals as experts in their own lives, viewing problems as separate from the person, and recognising that people have the skills, values, and strengths to reduce the impact of those problems (cited in Wallis et al., 2011). This definition captures the core principles of narrative therapy: externalising problems, empowering clients, and drawing on their existing capabilities. Narrative therapy is a

DOI: 10.4324/9781003584995-2

respectful, non-blaming approach that positions clients as the authors of their lives. It sees identity as distinct from problems and promotes the use of personal strengths to reshape one's narrative (Dulwich Centre, n.d.). According to the British Association for Counselling and Psychotherapy (BACP, n.d.), this approach encourages individuals to rewrite their stories in more empowering ways, fostering resilience and self- determination. As a strengths-based and collaborative model, narrative therapy supports clients, whether individuals, couples, or families, in recognising their capacity to live according to their values. During crises or trauma, it promotes a hopeful, future-oriented mindset, with the therapist acting as a supportive partner (Rice, 2015). The Narrative Therapy Centre (n.d.) further emphasises its non-pathologising and collaborative nature, acknowledging people's expertise and resources for change. It also considers broader social contexts, including class, race, gender, sexuality, and ability, recognising how these factors shape personal narratives and experiences.

Narrative therapy views problems as separate from the individual, reducing their personal impact. It empowers clients by recognising them as experts in their own lives and supports change through the development of strengths, skills, and values. This non-pathologising approach avoids labels, focusing instead on the broader context of clients' experiences. The process is collaborative, with therapist and client working together to reframe narratives. It also considers social factors such as race, gender, and class. By fostering hope and resilience –especially in times of crisis – narrative therapy helps individuals transform self-defeating stories into empowering ones. Common themes in narrative therapy are summarised in Table 1.1.

Table 1.1 Common themes in narrative therapy

Key theme	Explanation
Separation of problems	Viewing problems as distinct from the person, reducing their personal impact.
Client as expert	Clients are regarded as experts in their own lives, empowering them to guide change.
Focus on strengths	Emphasises the use of personal skills, competencies, and values to overcome obstacles.
Non-pathologising	Avoids labelling and diagnoses, focusing on understanding the broader context.
Collaborative process	The therapist and client work together to reframe and reconstruct personal narratives.
Contextual awareness	Considers individual context such as race, gender, class, and other life experiences.
Hope and resilience	Cultivates hope and encourages resilience, particularly in times of crisis.
Rewriting narratives	Helps individuals alter self-defeating stories into more empowering and positive ones.

Theoretical framework and assumptions

Narrative therapy is grounded in postmodern social constructionist theory, which emphasises language, social context, and self-determination in shaping human experience. Influenced by postmodernism, it challenges the notion of absolute truth, asserting that reality is subjective and constructed through language, culture, and history. Different people and cultures create different worldviews. Parry and Doan (1994, cited in Morris, 2006) state that narrative therapy assumes "there is no truth, only different interpretations of reality," with meaning shaped by social, cultural, and political contexts. Narrative therapy holds that people make sense of their lives through stories, which are not fixed but open to re-authoring. Identities are formed and reshaped through these narratives, which are influenced by language and social interaction.

A core principle of narrative therapy is separating the person from the problem. Problems are viewed as external influences rather than inherent traits, allowing individuals to see them as challenges rather than personal flaws. This externalisation reduces shame, guilt, and self-blame. Another key concept is re-authoring one's life narrative. By examining and deconstructing dominant, often negative, stories, clients can challenge limiting beliefs and highlight overlooked strengths, values, and abilities, fostering purpose, autonomy and self-determination. Language plays a vital role in this process. Beyond communication, it shapes identity and influences how people interpret their experiences. Language becomes a tool for transformation, enabling clients to reframe problems and envision new possibilities. For example, rather than saying "I am anxious" or "I have anxiety," a client might say, "Anxiety is something I struggle with," creating psychological distance and a more constructive outlook. Narrative therapy recognises that personal challenges are often shaped by broader social and cultural forces, including power dynamics related to race, class, gender, sexuality, and identity. It considers the wider context in which problems arise, such as environmental, relational, and cultural factors, to deepen understanding.

A key principle is its collaborative nature, where therapist and client work as equal partners. The therapist, acting as a facilitator, supports clients in exploring and reshaping their life stories without imposing interpretations. This client-centred, non-hierarchical approach values the client's expertise and lived experience. White and Epston (1990) emphasise respecting clients' views, separating the person from the problem, avoiding blame, and affirming the client's ability to address challenges. Narrative therapy is strengths-based, focusing on clients' skills and resources rather than deficits. By highlighting past strengths, it fosters resilience and hope, empowering clients to face current issues. Morgan (2000) describes narrative therapy as a respectful, non-blaming approach that empowers individuals as experts in their own lives. It separates the person from the problem, recognising inherent strengths, values, and abilities to change their relationship with challenges. Emphasising curiosity and open-ended exploration, the therapy process is collaboratively shaped by the client. Narrative therapy is flexible and empowering. It focuses on personal narratives, challenges dominant cultural discourses, and promotes a collaborative therapist–client relationship. Through externalisation, clients are supported in re-authoring their stories, fostering purpose, self-determination and hope.

Narrative therapy – the evidence

Narrative therapy has proven effective across various conditions and settings, benefiting individuals, families, and communities (Kelley, 2011). Research supports its use for a wide range of psychological and behavioural issues. It has shown positive outcomes in treating major depressive disorder (Vromans & Schweitzer, 2011), improving behaviour in children with ADHD (Looyeh et al., 2012), reducing psychological distress (Cashin et al., 2013), treating childhood social phobia (Looyeh et al., 2014), and managing PTSD (Erbes et al., 2014). It is especially helpful for those affected by adverse childhood experiences, domestic violence, attachment issues, and bullying (Lonne, 2015). Further studies highlight its role in enhancing empathy, decision-making, and social skills in children (Beaudoin et al., 2016); its recognition by the APA (American Psychological Association) as a treatment for PTSD (2017); and its effectiveness in reducing PTSD and depression symptoms (Lely et al., 2019). Narrative therapy has also shown benefits in treating depression and anxiety (Shakeri et al., 2020), improving marital satisfaction (Ghavibazou et al., 2020), restoring life wisdom (Chow & Fung, 2021), strengthening relationships and preventing conflict (Chimpén-López et al., 2021), addressing ADHD (Attention-Deficit/Hyperactivity Disorder) (Fatahi et al., 2021), and enhancing resilience among orphaned and abandoned children (Karibwendea et al., 2022). A recent study also found it significantly reduced loneliness through a phone-based, wisdom-focused intervention (Jiang et al., 2025). The evidence indicates that narrative therapy is a valuable approach for reframing experiences across a wide range of conditions. However, its long-term effectiveness compared to traditional therapies remains debated. Critics argue that its focus on storytelling may oversimplify complex issues by neglecting the interaction of multiple factors.

One concern is its strong foundation in social constructionism, which, while offering important insights, may overlook biological and neurological influences on mental health (NeuroLaunch Editorial Team, 2024). Positioning clients as experts can be challenging for those with cognitive limitations, and reframing alone may not fully address entrenched trauma or negative thought patterns. Cultural differences, lack of confidence, and communication barriers may also limit self-expression. Without a clear therapeutic agenda, the process can become unfocused. Since personal narratives are subjective, clients may unconsciously omit difficult truths or portray experiences more positively than they were. For those with limited language or emotional expression, narrative therapy may be less effective.

Another limitation lies in evaluating outcomes. Unlike approaches that use standardised measures, the success of narrative therapy is harder to quantify, making scientific assessment more complex (NeuroLaunch Editorial Team, 2024). Further research is needed to identify which mental health conditions narrative therapy treats most effectively. It is also important to explore how this approach works across different cultural groups, especially with Muslim clients. Future studies should examine both the overall effectiveness of narrative therapy and its cultural and religious relevance, particularly how these factors shape the therapeutic process.

Techniques used in narrative therapy

Narrative therapy uses various techniques to empower individuals and reshape their relationship with challenges. It focuses on building a strong therapeutic alliance, deconstructing problem-narratives, and co-authoring alternative stories that reflect the client's values and goals (Vromans & Schweitzer, 2015). This process supports embracing new narratives, promoting growth, self-determination, and transformation. Key techniques include narrative construction, externalisation, deconstruction, identifying unique outcomes, and existential exploration. Together, these methods help clients to re-author their lives and face challenges with resilience and confidence.

Telling one's story (putting together your narrative)

Narrative therapists help clients construct their stories, identifying dominant and problematic narratives in their own words. Storytelling shapes human experience, culture, and worldview, serving as a fundamental way to process information, connect socially, and create meaning (Ricoeur, 1984). It transmits cultural values and norms (Bascom, 1965), fosters moral imagination (Nussbaum, 1997), and holds transformative power for personal and collective change (Angus & McLeod, 2004; White & Epston, 1990). The process of telling one's story – often called "re-authoring" or "re-storying" – involves making sense of experiences and exploring different meanings. Narrative therapy encourages clients to recognise their power to create new meanings, understanding that a single event can be interpreted in many ways based on individual perspectives (Dulwich Centre, n.d.; Vinney, 2019).

Externalisation

After constructing the client's story, the therapist helps create psychological distance from their problems through externalisation. This technique separates the person from the issue, allowing clients to see problems as external rather than part of their identity. Bennet (2018) highlights that externalising the problem offers a clearer perspective, reducing self-blame and promoting empowerment. This distance helps clients focus on changing harmful behaviours instead of feeling overwhelmed or defined by them. For example, instead of saying, "I am an anxious person," a client might say, "Anxiety sometimes affects my life." This shift enables objective reflection and proactive change. Externalisation helps clients realise they are not powerless, fostering empowerment and self-determination by showing they can influence their thoughts, emotions, and behaviours to create meaningful change.

Deconstruction

Deconstruction is a vital phase in narrative therapy that helps clients clarify their stories. When overwhelmed by their narratives, clients work with the therapist to break their story into smaller, clearer parts (Wallis et al., 2011). This process uncovers the roots of their struggles. For example, someone feeling lonely might initially think their partner no longer cares, but deconstruction helps explore deeper causes and alternative explanations. This technique fosters a deeper understanding of underlying issues by examining stressful events or patterns, empowering clients to gain insight and confidence in addressing their challenges.

Unique outcomes

Unique outcomes in narrative therapy highlight exceptions to dominant negative stories, offering openings for new, positive narratives and therapeutic change (Gonçalves et al., 2009). Clients often get stuck in negative patterns, and therapists help them explore alternative interpretations. Since experiences can be seen in many ways, discovering different perspectives builds clients' confidence to overcome challenges. This process promotes growth, resilience, and a renewed sense of control over their lives.

Existentialism

Existential therapy focuses on exploring what it means to be human, helping clients face life's challenges with meaning. According to Iacovou & Weixel-Dixon (2015), it clarifies personal values, goals, and relationships. A common method within narrative therapy is phenomenological therapy, defined by Van Deurzen (2015) as a systematic description of conscious awareness that uncovers universal meanings by setting aside assumptions and biases. This approach allows clients to openly explore their perceptions and experiences, helping them find clearer meaning and purpose. Rather than imposing interpretations, existential therapy supports clients in constructing their own life narratives based on lived experience.

Conclusions

Narrative therapy, grounded in social constructionism and postmodernism, highlights language's role in shaping identity and meaning. It effectively addresses trauma, low self-esteem, depression, PTSD, anxiety, learning disabilities, eating disorders, and family conflicts. Core techniques include externalising problems, deconstruction, identifying unique outcomes, meaning-making, and challenging unhelpful discourses. These help clients reshape their narratives, promoting positive change and growth. A central principle is externalising problems, separating the individual from their issues to reduce helplessness and self-blame. Research shows that proper use of these techniques enhances effectiveness (Ghavibazou et al., 2020). By shifting focus from blame to meaning, clients find healthier ways to face challenges. Therapists collaborate with clients as experts of their own lives, fostering autonomy and self-discovery. Clients learn to align their lives with their values and aspirations in a supportive, non-judgemental space. Narrative therapy acknowledges cultural, social, and political influences, helping clients reframe experiences, uncover hidden strengths, and build resilience. It moves away from pathology towards empowerment and personal meaning.

References

American Psychological Association. (2017). *Narrative Exposure Therapy (NET). Clinical Practice Guideline for the Treatment of Posttraumatic Stress Disorder (PTSD).* https://www.apa.org/ptsd-guideline/treatments/narrative-exposure-therapy

Angus, L. E., & McLeod, J. (2004). *The handbook of narrative and psychotherapy: Practice, theory, and research.* Sage Publications.

BACP. (n.d.). *Types of therapy: Narrative therapy.* British Association for Counselling and Psychotherapy. https://www.bacp.co.uk/about-therapy/types-of-therapy/narrative-therapy

Bascom, W. (1965). The forms of folklore: Prose narratives. *Journal of American Folklore, 78*(307), 3–20. https://www.jstor.org/stable/i223643.

Beaudoin, M., Moersch, M., & Evare, B. S. (2016). The effectiveness of narrative therapy with children's social and emotional skill development: An empirical study of 813 problem-solving stories. *Journal of Systemic Therapies, 35*(3), 42–59.

Bennet, T. (2018). *Externalization narrative therapy: Separate yourself from your problems.* https://thriveworks.com/blog/externalizing-problem-counseling-technique-narrative-therapy/

Cashin, A., Browne, G., Bradbury, J., & Mulder, A. (2013). The effectiveness of narrative therapy with young people with autism. *Journal of Child and Adolescent Psychiatric Nursing, 26*(1), 32–41.

Chimpén-López, C. A., Pacheco, M., Pretel-Luque, T., Bastón, R., & Chimpén-Sagrado, D. (2021). The couple's tree of life: Promoting and protecting relational identity. *Family Process, 00*, 1–14. https://doi.org/10.1111/famp.12727.

Chow, E. O. W., & Fung, S-F. (2021). Narrative group intervention to rediscover life wisdom among Hong Kong Chinese older adults: A Single-blind randomized waitlist-controlled trial. *Oxford University Press on Behalf of the Gerontological Society of America.* https://doi.org/10.1093/geroni/igab027.

Deurzen, E. van. (2015). Phenomenological therapy. In E. Neukrug (Ed.), *The SAGE encyclopedia of theory in counseling and psychotherapy* (Vol. 2, pp. 772–776). Sage Publication.

Dulwich Centre. (n.d.). *Narrative therapy: An overview.* https://dulwichcentre.com.au/what-is-narrative-therapy/

Erbes, C. R., Stillman, J. R., Wieling, E., Bera, W., & Leskela, J. (2014). A pilot examination of the use of narrative therapy with individuals diagnosed with PTSD. Journal of Traumatic Stress, 27(6), 730–733.

Fatahi, N., Bardideh, M., Talebi Bahman Biglou, R., Gholami, Z., Akbarinejad, M., & Hoshyar, N. (2021). The effectiveness of narrative therapy on reducing behavior problems and improving self-perception in students. *Quarterly Journal of Child Mental Health, 7*(4), 297–312. https://dx.doi.org/10.52547/jcmh.7.4.19.

Ghavibazou, E., Hosseinian, S., & Abdollahi, A. (2020). Effectiveness of narrative therapy on communication patterns for women experiencing low marital satisfaction. *Australian & New Zealand Journal of Family Therapy, 41*(2), 195–207.

Gonçalves, M. M., Matos, M., & Santos, A. (2009). Narrative therapy and the nature of "Innovative Moments" in the construction of change. *Journal of Constructivist Psychology, 22*(1), 1–23.

Harms, L. (2007). *Working with people: Communication skills for reflective practice.* Oxford University Press.

Iacovou, S., & Weixel-Dixon, K. (2015). *Existential therapy: 100 Key points and techniques.* Routledge.

Jiang, D., Tang, V. F. Y., Kahlon, M., Chow, E. O., Yeung, D. Y., Aubrey, R., & Chou, K. L. (2025). Effects of wisdom-enhancement narrative-therapy and empathy-focused interventions on loneliness over 4 weeks among older adults: A randomized controlled trial. *The American Journal of Geriatric Psychiatry: Official Journal of the American Association for Geriatric Psychiatry, 33*(1), 18–30. https://doi.org/10.1016/j.jagp.2024.07.003.

Karibwendea, F., Niyonsengaa, J., Nyirinkwayac, S. et al. (2022). A randomized controlled trial evaluating the effectiveness of narrative therapy on resilience of orphaned and abandoned children fostered in SOS children's village. *European Journal of Psychotraumatology*, 13, 2152111. https://doi.org/10.1080/20008066.2022.2152111.

Kelley, P. (2011). Narrative theory and social work treatment. In F. Turner (Ed.), Social work treatment: Interlocking theoretical approaches (5th ed., pp. 315–326). Oxford University Press.

Lely, J. C., Smid, G. E., Jongedijk, R. A., Knipscheer, J. W., & Kleber, R. J. (2019). The effectiveness of narrative exposure therapy: A review, meta-analysis, and meta-regression analysis. *European Journal of Psychotraumatology, 10*(1), 1550344. https://doi.org/10.1080/20008198.2018.1550344.

Lonne, B. (2015). *Narrative therapy practice. Slides from lecture at University of New England, Armidale, Australia in the unit HSSW410 – social work interventions – models and skills.* Cited in The Social Work Graduate, Resources for social work graduates. Various social work practice approaches. https://www. thesocialworkgraduate.com/post/narrative-therapy

Looyeh, M. Y., Kamali, K., Ghasemi, A., & Tonawanik, P. (2014). Treating social phobia in children through group narrative therapy. *The Arts in Psychotherapy, 41*(1), 16–20.

Looyeh, M. Y., Kamali, K., & Shafieian, R. (2012). An exploratory study of the effectiveness of group narrative therapy on the school behavior of girls with attention-deficit/hyperactivity symptoms. *Archives of Psychiatric Nursing, 26*(5), 404–410.

Morgan, A. (2000). *What is narrative therapy? An easy-to-read introduction*. Dulwich Centre Publications.

Morris, C. C. (2006). *Narrative theory: A culturally sensitive counseling and research framework*. https://www.semanticscholar.org/paper/Narrative-Theory%3A-A-Culturally-Sensitive-Counseling-Morris/30833a4a0c3c539dc40e09f1149aaadbec738eb2

NeuroLaunch Editorial Team (2024). *Narrative therapy limitations: Exploring challenges and critiques*. https://neurolaunch.com/narrative-therapy-limitations/

Nussbaum, M. C. (1997). *Poetic justice: The literary imagination and public life*. Beacon Press.

Parry, A., & Doan, R. E. (1994). *Story re-visions: Narrative therapy in the postmodern world*. Guilford Press.

Rice, R. H. (2015). Narrative therapy. *The Sage Encyclopedia of Theory in Counseling and Psychology, 2*, 695–700.

Ricoeur, P. (1984). *Time and narrative* (Vol. 1). University of Chicago Press.

Shakeri, J., Ahmadi, S. M., Maleki, F., Hesami, M. R., Parsa Moghadam, A., Ahmadzade, A., Shirzadi, M., & Elahi, A. (2020). Effectiveness of group narrative therapy on depression, quality of life, and anxiety in people with amphetamine addiction: A randomized clinical trial. *Iran Journal of Medical Science, 45*(2), 91–99.

Vinney, C. (2019). *Understanding social identity theory and its impact on behavior.* ThoughCo. Web.

Vromans, L., & Schweitzer, R. D. (2015). *Narrative therapy. Encyclopedia of clinical psychology*. John Wiley & Sons. https://doi.org/10.1002/9781118625392.wbecp215

Vromans, L. P., & Schweitzer, R. D. (2011). Narrative therapy for adults with major depressive disorder: improved symptom and interpersonal outcomes. *Psychotherapy Research: Journal of the Society for Psychotherapy Research, 21*(1), 4–15. https://doi.org/10.1080/10503301003591792.

Wallis, J., Burns, J., & Capdevila, R. (2011). What is narrative therapy and what is it not? The usefulness of Q methodology to explore accounts of White and Epston's (1990) approach to narrative therapy. *Clinical Psychology & Psychotherapy, 18*(6), 486–497.

White, M., & Epston, D. (1990). *Narrative means to therapeutic ends*. Norton & Company.

White, M., & Epston, D. (2009). *Narrative means to therapeutic ends*. W. W. Norton.

2 Process and therapeutic conversation in narrative therapy

Introduction

The narrative therapist plays a crucial role in creating a supportive environment where clients feel heard, validated, and empowered to explore their life stories. Rather than an authority, the therapist acts as a compassionate collaborator, guiding clients to uncover the meanings shaping their experiences. They facilitate self-discovery by helping clients see how cultural, societal, and familial discourses influence their narratives. Offering a non-judgemental, empathetic space, the therapist supports clients in examining and externalising problems entangled with their identity. In Islāmic Integrated Narrative Therapy, the therapist's role expands to include integrating Islāmic values, principles, and teachings. The therapist helps clients reconcile their experiences with faith, fostering healing and narrative transformation consistent with Islāmic beliefs. Core techniques, narrative construction, externalisation, deconstruction, unique outcomes, and existentialism (as appropriate) are applied clinically to empower clients to reshape their stories in line with personal values and aspirations. These methods equip clients to break limiting patterns and create authentic, empowering narratives. This chapter examines the therapist's role and explores clinical use of key techniques, illustrating how externalisation, deconstruction, unique outcomes, and existentialism are applied in practice.

The role of the narrative therapist

Narrative therapy is client-centred, tailoring the process to each individual's unique experiences and worldview. While primarily non-directive, it uses guiding techniques like externalisation, deconstruction, and exploring unique outcomes. Active listening is essential, involving full attention to clients' words, emotions, and underlying themes. For example, a therapist attentively listens to a client's traumatic story without interruption, helping them feel validated and understood – laying the groundwork for deeper reflection.

DOI: 10.4324/9781003584995-3

Empathy is vital in narrative therapy, defined as the therapist's ability to understand the client's thoughts and feelings from their perspective (Rassool, 2025, p. 113). The therapist acts as a mirror, fostering self-exploration and creating a safe, supportive space for growth. Watson (2002) highlights that full empathy includes understanding both meaning and emotion, which is crucial for client progress. She states, "When empathy operates on interpersonal, cognitive, and affective levels, it is one of the most powerful tools therapists have" (pp. 463–464). Empathy builds trust, allowing clients to explore sensitive issues safely. For instance, responding to trauma with, "I can hear how difficult that must have been for you," validates emotions and promotes healing. A non-judgemental approach in narrative therapy means the therapist avoids labelling, interpreting, or assuming about the client's experiences. Instead, they create a safe space where clients feel heard, valued, and free to explore their stories without fear of criticism. For example, rather than saying, "That was a bad decision," the therapist might ask, "Tell me more about what led to that decision." This openness helps clients explore their narrative without shame. Narrative therapists use deep, reflective questions to encourage new perspectives, such as "What would your life look like if this problem didn't define you?" or "Can you recall a time you acted differently than this story suggests?" These questions help reveal alternative narratives that emphasise strengths and potential for change.

In narrative therapy, the therapist partners with the client, working collaboratively rather than directing or controlling the process. The therapist avoids imposing solutions or judgements, instead supporting clients to explore, externalise, and deconstruct their narratives to discover new meanings and possibilities. For example, a therapist might ask, "What do you think would be a helpful next step?" to encourage client agency and empowerment. This collaborative relationship helps both parties work towards improving the client's narrative outcomes. Therapists guide clients in critically examining their life stories, highlighting how cultural and societal factors, like gender roles or family expectations, shape their views. This process challenges limiting beliefs and opens new possibilities. Deconstruction breaks down complex or overwhelming stories into manageable parts, fostering clarity, understanding, and emotional regulation. For instance, with grief, a therapist might focus on specific memories or support systems rather than the entire loss at once. If a client says, "I'm not good at relationships," the therapist might explore what a "good" relationship means to them, identify moments of connection, and consider external influences shaping that belief. This helps clients recognise their strengths and positive experiences. By breaking experiences into smaller parts, therapists empower clients to identify patterns, challenge limiting beliefs, and gradually rebuild narratives that support healing and growth.

In narrative therapy, the therapist acts as a facilitator, with the client leading and possessing greater insight into their own problems. Morris (2006) described the counsellor's role as that of a cultural anthropologist, approaching the client's stories with curiosity and "not knowing," encouraging reflection on the narratives shaping their lives. Rather than imposing interpretations, the therapist supports clients in reshaping their personal stories, enabling new perspectives, problem externalisation, and empowering narratives. For example, when a client feels defined by depression, the therapist might say, "Instead of seeing yourself as 'depressed,' how has depression affected your life?" This externalisation helps clients view problems as separate forces they can confront, reducing self-blame and opening space for change. As facilitators, therapists ask thoughtful questions to reveal overlooked experiences and strengths. A client stuck in an unfulfilling job who labels themselves "unambitious" may be guided to explore their values and goals, fostering a new, positive self-narrative that encourages growth and action. Therapists also help uncover hidden strengths by reflecting on moments of resilience and competence. For instance, after hearing about a challenging work situation, the therapist might say, "You showed real resilience handling that stress," reinforcing the client's abilities and shifting focus to strengths. Finally, narrative therapists empower clients by positioning them as the experts and authors of their stories. For a client feeling helpless in a relationship, the therapist assists in reframing their narrative, identifying needs, and setting boundaries, helping them make decisions aligned with their values. This process transforms clients from passive victims into active agents of change, boosting self-efficacy and confidence.

In narrative therapy, cycles of reflection play a crucial role in helping clients gain deeper insight into their emotional responses, thought patterns, and behaviours. Reflective practices encourage self-awareness by allowing individuals to step back and examine their narratives from different perspectives. This process helps clients recognise how dominant cultural and societal discourses have shaped their identities and beliefs, enabling them to reconstruct more empowering personal stories. Reflective practices in narrative therapy may include:

- Externalising problems
- Reflective questioning
- Re-authoring narratives
- Therapeutic letter writing
- Journaling

Through reflective practices, narrative therapy becomes a transformative process, helping clients develop deeper insight into their emotions and behaviours. This self-awareness supports healing and personal growth. Narrative therapists offer emotional support by guiding clients through the emotional impact of their stories. For instance, a grieving client may feel overwhelmed by sadness; the therapist provides compassionate presence, listens without judgement, and helps them integrate the loss into a new narrative of resilience and healing. This supportive role fosters a safe environment for emotional

Table 2.1 Roles of a narrative therapist

Role	Description
Client-centred approach	The therapy focuses on the individual's unique experiences, empowering them to take ownership of their narrative and create meaningful change.
Active listener	Deeply listens to the client's stories without judgement or imposing interpretations, creating a safe space for them to open up.
Empathy	Empathy is essential for creating a compassionate environment where clients feel heard and understood.
Non-judgemental	A non-judgemental approach ensures that clients can explore their stories freely without fear of criticism.
Collaborator	Works alongside the client as an equal partner rather than an authority figure.
Guiding	Guiding individuals in examining their narratives and recognising the impact of cultural and societal discourses on their perspectives.
Facilitator of externalisation	Assists clients in separating their identity from their problems.
Facilitator of narrative	Enabling clients in exploring and creating new, empowering interpretations of their experiences. Assists clients in reshaping their stories to align with their values and aspirations.
Deconstructor	Helps challenge and deconstruct limiting beliefs, narratives, and dominant discourses that negatively impact the client's sense of self.
Facilitator of strengths	Highlights the client's abilities, skills, competencies, resilience, and unique outcomes.
Facilitator of reflection	Encourages clients to pause and reflect on their stories, helping them gain insight into their beliefs, behaviours, and emotional responses.
Facilitator of empowerment	Empowers clients to take control of their life narratives and enables an individual to make independent choices, take actions, and influence their own lives.
Support	Providing compassionate support to individuals as they navigate the emotional effects of their narratives, offering guidance, empathy, and a safe space for them to process and transform their experiences.

expression and meaningful transformation. The roles of a narrative therapist are presented in Table 2.1.

The key significant roles of the narrative therapist include (Adapted from The Social Work Graduate)

- "To bring about change by analysing problematic stories, i.e., stories that reveal problems that disempower people.
- To externalise people's problems, i.e., they discuss the problem as an issue in itself rather than something linked to the person.

- To deconstruct negative/problem-based stories in order to uncover alternative views, reinforcing a person's strengths.
- Use these alternative views to reconstruct positive stories that can empower.
- Encourage the client to share these positive stories with others as they live out these new stories."

A core principle of narrative therapy is the rejection of diagnostic labelling. Unlike traditional psychological models that emphasise diagnoses such as depression or anxiety disorders, narrative therapy separates the person from the problem. This distinction is essential, as labels can lead clients to internalise negative identities, potentially reinforcing feelings of helplessness. For example, a client labelled as "depressed" may come to see themselves as inherently flawed or incapable of change. Instead, narrative therapy promotes the idea that individuals are not defined by their problems. The therapeutic relationship is grounded in the therapist's attitudes and competence, with an emphasis on empathy, respect, and collaboration. The approach is non-judgemental and avoids victim-blaming, focusing instead on understanding the client's experiences with openness and curiosity. Ultimately, the aim is to help clients enhance their self-understanding and reshape their worldview in empowering ways.

Process and therapeutic conversations in narrative therapy

In narrative therapy, assessment differs fundamentally from traditional approaches by focusing on exploration rather than diagnosis. Instead of identifying symptoms or assigning labels, the process centres on discovery through storytelling and conversation. A key technique is externalisation, where problems are viewed as separate from the individual (Parry & Doan, 1994), allowing clients to see their issues as influences in their lives rather than as intrinsic flaws. Early sessions involve clients sharing their stories, followed by carefully structured questioning to understand the problem's impact. Narrative therapists use various skills – including empathetic listening, open and closed questions, clarification, paraphrasing, probing, and summarising – to facilitate the therapeutic process. Language is treated as a powerful tool for change. Therapists ask questions from a stance of curiosity, not as experts but as co-explorers (Goolishian & Anderson, 1992). As Laube (1998) states, "Narrative therapists explore the variety of effects of problems on people's lives and distinguish the meaning a problem has acquired in a person's life from the person himself or herself" (p. 231). This non-pathologising approach allows clients to reframe their experiences and develop empowering narratives.

Narrative therapy employs a range of techniques and exercises (see Table 2.2) that focus on reshaping the client's relationship with their problems.

Table 2.2 Techniques, corresponding questions, and examples

Techniques	Questions	Examples
Externalisation questions	*"If this problem were a character in your story, what would it look like? How would you describe its influence on your life?"*	A client struggling with anger might be asked, *"When anger shows up, what does it want you to do? How does it affect your relationships?"*
Deconstruction questions	*"Where do you think this idea about yourself comes from? Who or what shaped it?"*	A client who believes *"I'm unworthy"* could be asked, *"What experiences or messages taught you this? Are there other ways to interpret those experiences?"*
Re-authoring questions	*"What strengths have you demonstrated in overcoming this challenge?"*	A client recovering from failure might be asked, *"Despite this setback, what does your persistence say about you?"*
Unique outcomes	*"Can you think of a time when this problem didn't control you? What was different then?"*	A client with low confidence might be asked, *"Tell me about a moment when you felt capable, what did that experience teach you?"*
Letter writing	*"If you could write a letter to your problem, what would you say to it?"*	A letter to their childhood self about overcoming adversity.
Journalling	*"If your journey were recorded, what title would you give this chapter of your life?"*	A client writes a journal entry about moments when they felt empowered and capable.
Support	*"Who in your life can support your new narrative?"*	A recovering addict might be encouraged to share their growth story with a supportive group.
Empowerment	*"How would it feel to have people reflect back your new identity?"*	A structured event where others affirm the client's evolving story. Family members recognising a client's transformation.

Core components of this approach include building a strong therapeutic alliance, deconstructing problem-saturated stories, constructing alternative and preferred identities, and supporting clients in living these new narratives. As Vromans and Schweitzer (2015) note, narrative therapy "is respectful of different cultural understandings of well-being and healing," and values the importance of witnessing and community, often extending its reach into marginalised contexts globally. Key techniques used in narrative therapy include story construction, externalisation, deconstruction, identifying unique outcomes, deep questioning, letter writing, and journalling. Deep questioning plays a central role in this process, encouraging clients to critically reflect on their experiences and re-author their narratives. These include externalising questions, deconstructive questions, and re-authoring questions, all designed to help clients distance themselves from their problems, challenge limiting beliefs, and construct more empowering self-identities. Through this reflective process, clients not only gain insight but also develop a stronger sense of agency, recognising that they are not defined by their difficulties.

In narrative therapy, the process of constructing one's story often reveals a problem-saturated description, a dominant narrative that contributes to the client's distress. Effective listening and careful questioning are essential at this stage, enabling the therapist to gather a detailed history of the problem while considering the client's thoughts, beliefs, and social context (Payne, 2006). Using the client's own language is vital, as it fosters a collaborative and reflective process that helps clarify key issues within their narrative. During the stage of externalisation, the therapist may invite the client to name the problem (e.g., "anger" or "worry"), encouraging them to view it as separate from their identity. This technique empowers clients by giving them greater control over their experiences (Bishop, 2011). The therapist consistently refers to the issue by its given name, often personifying it as "it" or "the," which reinforces the idea of the problem as an external force (Bennet, 2018). For instance, instead of saying, "I am stressed," the client might say, "I am currently living with stress." The therapist may then ask, "When did you first notice the presence of stress?" – guiding the client towards recognising how the problem has influenced their life. This process supports clients in taking steps to change unhelpful behaviours and reshape their narrative.

The Dulwich Centre (2022) suggests an initial discussion of four areas that will aid therapists to externalise the problem:

- Characterise the problem in an experience-near way. Listen as the person talks about the problem.
- Connect the problem to its antecedents, effects, links with others, etc.
- Have the person describe their experience of and position on the effects of the problem.
- Locate this experience and position within the person's wider values.

With repeated practice, externalising the problem empowers clients to shift their focus towards changing unwanted behaviours. For instance, a client might personify their anxiety as "theGoblin," describing how they feel when "the Goblin" appears and how they manage its presence (Rice, 2015). When clients have lived with a problematic narrative for a long time, it can feel overwhelming or irresolvable. These emotions often lead to overgeneralised statements, reinforcing and amplifying the issue. Deconstruction helps by breaking down complex problems into smaller, clearer elements, making them more manageable. Narrative therapists guide clients in dissecting their stories to uncover the core issues and increase insight. For example, consider a couple experiencing relationship difficulties. One partner expresses frustration that the other rarely shares her thoughts or emotions. At first glance, the problem is vague and difficult to address. Through deconstruction, the therapist would help both partners explore the underlying dynamics, communication patterns, and unspoken expectations, leading to a clearer understanding and potential resolution.

To deconstruct the problem, a therapist might ask questions such as:

- *"Can you recall specific instances when you felt unheard or disconnected?"*
- *"Has your partner always been this way, or has something changed over time?"*
- *"What does 'not sharing' mean to you? Are there particular topics or situations where this is most noticeable?"*
- *"How do you typically respond when your partner does not express her thoughts or feelings?"*
- *"Are there moments when she does share, even in small ways? What makes those situations different?"*

These questions help break down the problem into manageable parts, making it easier to understand and address. This process often reveals deeper issues, such as hidden feelings of loneliness or a desire for emotional connection. A client may initially frame their story as being a victim of an unfulfilling relationship, but through deconstruction, they may come to recognise the core issue as difficulty expressing vulnerability or coping with isolation. Importantly, deconstruction also considers the religious, socio-cultural, and political contexts that shape the client's experiences and beliefs, allowing for a more holistic understanding of the problem. Once clarity is achieved through deconstructing the dominant narrative, the therapy process progresses to the reconstruction phase, where clients begin to build new, empowering stories that reflect their values, strengths, and aspirations. To facilitate narrative reconstruction, O'Connor et al. (2008) suggest the following steps to facilitate narrative reconstruction:

- Uncover the narratives: Identify dominant, devalued, and key player narratives.
- Identify narrative functions: Understand the roles of different narratives in the client's life.
- Validate narratives: Acknowledge the significance of the identified narratives.
- Build alternative narratives (re-authoring): Construct new narratives that empower the client.
- Retell the story in a new way (re-storying): Narrate the client's story in an empowering manner.
- Create further social validation: Establish an audience that supports the new narratives.

This process enables clients to explore the depth of their problems, identify specific threats, and reflect on the influence of religious, socio-cultural, and political contexts on their experiences (O'Connor et al., 2008). By doing so, clients gain a clearer understanding of the problem and the challenges it poses. The unique outcomes technique in narrative therapy focuses on identifying moments when the client's actions or experiences diverged from their dominant problem-story. These often subtle, overlooked moments can highlight a client's strengths, resilience, or agency (Bishop, 2011). Re-authoring one's narrative begins with recognising these exceptions, times when the problem did not take control. Therapists listen closely for these exceptions during conversations and inquire further by asking questions about the skills, values, or intentions demonstrated in those moments. This aligns with the core idea that individuals can actively re-author their lives, reinforcing their capacity for change and growth (AIPC, 2010). For example, therapists may ask:

- *"Can you recall a time when this problem did not feel overwhelming? What was different then?"*
- *"How did you handle things in that situation? What does that reveal about you?"*

The contents of these narratives are explored by the therapist and client to identify the circumstances or context surrounding the unique outcome to understand what made it possible. Questions might include:

- *"Who was there with you at that time, and how did they support you?"*
- *"What thoughts or actions helped your success in that situation?"*

Once a unique outcome is identified, therapists help the client explore how it aligns with their personal values, goals, or sense of identity. The therapist encourages the client to integrate these alternative stories into their broader narrative. For instance, imagine a client struggling with a belief that they are "always anxious." Through conversation, the therapist uncovers a moment when the client managed a stressful situation effectively despite feeling anxious. This unique outcome might then be explored:

- *What helped them manage that situation?*
- *What strengths or coping strategies does this reflect?*
- *How might they apply this approach to other anxiety-provoking situations?*

This technique empowers clients to recognise their capacity to manage anxiety, emphasising their strengths and past successes. It supports a narrative shift from seeing themselves as "always anxious" to viewing themselves as capable and resilient in the face of challenges. One therapeutic approach that may be integrated with narrative therapy is the use of existential interventions. However, there is ongoing debate within existential therapy regarding the use of structured techniques. Some existential therapists, particularly purists, eschew technical interventions, arguing that such methods may compromise the authenticity and integrity of the therapeutic relationship (Ackerman, 2017). Despite this stance, many existential practitioners incorporate interventions from other modalities, such as psychoanalysis, CBT (cognitive behavioural therapy), solution-focused therapy, person-centred therapy, and Gestalt therapy. These are applied in ways that align with existential therapy's core principles, particularly its emphasis on personal responsibility, authenticity, and the client's engagement with existence (van Deurzen, 2012). For a more detailed exploration of existential theory and practice, key texts include Adams (2013) and Deurzen & Adams (2016), which offer comprehensive insights into existential thought and its application in psychotherapy.

Narrative therapy uses various tools to help clients reshape their stories. Therapeutic documents like letters and notes record progress and insights. Re-membering reflects on important people, past or present. Rituals and celebrations mark key therapeutic milestones. Outsider-witnesses, such as family, friends, or peers, offer validation and support. The "Tree of Life" employs a tree metaphor to explore identity and life experiences. These techniques empower clients to create meaningful, hopeful narratives. A summary of the various tools and examples is presented in Table 2.3.

Table 2.3 Narrative therapy tools and examples

Tool	Examples
Therapeutic documents	Written documents such as declarations, certificates, handbooks, letters, session notes, films, lists, and photos. These documents summarise a person's discoveries, highlight progress, and reinforce their evolving narrative.
Re-membering	Reflecting on memories of significant people, including strangers who made a positive impact and famous figures whose courage or integrity has influenced the person's life.
Rituals and celebrations	Marking significant milestones in a person's therapeutic journey, often included at the conclusion of therapy to acknowledge progress and transformation.
Outsider-witnesses	Inviting family, friends, professionals, or individuals with similar experiences to witness and validate the client's progress. Their presence helps translate therapeutic insights into real-life action (Carey & Russell, 2003).
The Tree of Life	A creative exercise using a tree as a metaphor for one's life story. Clients reflect on different parts of the tree-roots, trunk, branches, leaves-to symbolise aspects of their past, present, and future (Dulwich Centre, 2009).

Source: Adapted from the Social Work Graduate.

Conclusion

Therapeutic conversations in narrative therapy focus on curiosity, empathy, and deep engagement with clients' stories. Therapists adopt a non-judgemental, open-ended stance, using thoughtful questions and active listening to understand the client's perspective. Building trust through empathy and reflective responses helps clients feel valued and heard. The process supports clients in exploring their narratives, identifying key themes, and enriching their experiences. A core aim is to challenge limiting stories and reveal empowering alternatives. Clients critically examine dominant beliefs shaping their identity and highlight moments when problems did not define them. Together, therapist and client co-create new, meaningful stories aligned with personal values and strengths. This collaboration often involves "thickening the plot" to deepen narratives and celebrating successes to reinforce positive change. Narrative therapy also prioritises client autonomy, cultural sensitivity, and respect for indigenous contexts.

References

Ackerman, C. E. (2017). *9 best narrative therapy techniques & worksheets [+PDF]*. https://positivepsychology.com/narrative-therapy/

Adams, M. (2013). *A concise introduction to existential counselling*. SAGE.

AIPC. (2010). Narrative therapy. https://www.aipc.net.au/articles/narrative-therapy/#:~:text=The%20most%20important%20aspect%20of%20Narrative%20Therapy%20is,the%20therapeutic%20relationship%2C%20in%20particular%20the%20therapist%E2%80%99s%20attitudes

Bennet, T. (2018). *Externalization narrative therapy: Separate yourself from your problems*. https://thriveworks.com/blog/externalizing-problem-counseling-technique-narrative-therapy/

Bishop, W. H. (2011, May 16). Narrative therapy summary. Thoughts From a Therapist. http://www.thoughtsfromatherapist.com/2011/05/16/narrative-therapy-summary/

Carey, M., & Russell, S. (2003). Re-Authoring: Some answers to commonly asked questions. *The International Journal of Narrative Therapy and Community Work, 3*, 19–43.

Deurzen, E. van. (2012). *Existential counselling and psychotherapy in practice*. Revised Third Edition. Sage Publications.

Deurzen, E. van, & Adams, M. (2016). *Skills in existential counselling & psychotherapy*. SAGE.

Dulwich Centre. (2009). The "tree of life" in a community context. *CONTEXT, 105*, 50–54. https://dulwichcentre.com.au/wp-content/uploads/2014/01/tree-of-life-community-context.pdf

Dulwich Centre (2022). *Muslim contributions to narrative therapy and community work*. https://dulwichcentre.com.au/muslim-contributions-to-narrative-therapy-and-community-work/

Goolishian, H. A., & Anderson, H. (1992). Strategy and intervention versus nonintervention. *Journal of Marital and Family Therapy, 18*(1), 5–15.

Laube, J. J. (1998). Therapist role in narrative group psychotherapy. *Group, 22*(4), 227–243.

Morris, C. C. (2006). *Narrative theory: A culturally sensitive counseling and research framework.* https://www.counselingoutfitters.com/Morris.htm

O'Connor, I., Wilson, J., Setterlund, D., & Hughes, M. (2008). *Social work and human service practice* (5th ed.). Pearson Education.

Parry, A., & Doan, R. E. (1994). *Story re-visions: Narrative therapy in the postmodern world.* Guilford Press.

Payne, M. (2006). *Narrative therapy: An introduction for counsellors* (2nd ed.). Sage Publications Ltd.

Rassool, G. Hussein. (2025). *Islāmic counselling & psychotherapy: An introduction to theory and practice* (pp. 110–127). Routledge.

Rice, R. H. (2015). Narrative therapy. *The SAGE Encyclopedia of Theory in Counseling and Psychology, 2,* 695–700.

The Social Work Graduate, *Resources for social work graduates. Various social work practice approaches.* https://www.thesocialworkgraduate.com/post/narrative-therapy

Vromans, L., & Schweitzer, R. D. (2015). *Narrative therapy. Encyclopedia of clinical psychology.* John Wiley & Sons. https://doi.org/10.1002/9781118625392.wbecp215

Watson, J. C. (2002). Re-visioning empathy'. In D. J. Cain & J. Seeman (Eds.), *Humanistic psychotherapies: Handbook of research and practice* (pp. 445–471). American Psychological Association.

3 Narrative therapy and Islāmic worldview

Conflict, harmony, and integration

Introduction

The application of Western psychotherapeutic methods without cultural and indigenous adaptation risks misrepresenting or overlooking the spiritual and cultural expressions of distress in Muslim clients. Therapists must consider how their approaches align with the epistemological (knowledge sources), ontological (nature of reality), and axiological (values and ethics) foundations of the Islāmic worldview. These foundations shape how suffering and healing are understood. Ignoring them may make interventions seem irrelevant or harmful to Muslim clients. As Willig (2019) emphasises, therapists should be aware of their basic assumptions about human nature (ontology) and how to understand clients' experiences (epistemology) (p. 186). Therefore, therapists need to assess whether their methods fit the Islāmic worldview before applying them.

For many Muslims, psychological distress extends beyond neurobiological or environmental causes, often stemming from spiritual disconnection or misalignment with divine principles. Overlooking these spiritual aspects can lead to an incomplete understanding of the client's inner experience and impede growth and healing. Therapeutic models that disregard spirituality, downplay divine will, or rely solely on secular, materialist frameworks may fall short of meeting the holistic needs of Muslim clients. Consequently, therapists must thoughtfully adapt existing approaches or seek alternative models aligned with Islāmic teachings. Narrative therapy, which centres on re-authoring personal stories, shows promise within Islāmic psychotherapy but demands careful scrutiny to ensure its compatibility with Islāmic epistemology, ontology, and axiology. This critical evaluation guarantees that interventions are both effective and spiritually coherent. Integrating Islāmic philosophical foundations into therapy underscores the unity of mental, emotional, moral, and spiritual well-being. By addressing these interconnected dimensions, therapists provide a more holistic, meaningful experience that affirms faith, enhances purpose, and fosters inner harmony. This chapter aims to examine whether narrative therapy's epistemological, ontological, and

DOI: 10.4324/9781003584995-4

axiological underpinnings align with the Islāmic worldview and how such alignment influences its relevance and efficacy for Muslim clients.

Narrative therapy and Islāmic beliefs and psychotherapy: epistemological, ontological, and axiological foundations

Narrative therapy and Islāmic psychotherapy (Rassool, 2025a, 2025b, 2025c) both aim to understand human experience but are founded on distinct philosophical and spiritual traditions. Their epistemological, ontological, and axiological bases shape their views on psychological distress, well-being, healing, and therapeutic practice. While some areas of overlap exist, significant tensions arise from their differing roots: narrative therapy is grounded in postmodern, secular ideals, whereas Islāmic psychotherapy is firmly embedded in religious and spiritual principles.

Narrative therapy is founded on postmodern epistemology, which rejects a single objective truth and instead views knowledge as socially constructed. Individuals create meaning through language, relationships, and cultural context, leading to multiple, equally valid interpretations of reality shaped by personal experience and social environment. Ontologically, it embraces constructivism, seeing reality as dynamic, subjective, and co-created. People are active agents shaping their identities through stories and interactions, able to reframe past events and re-author their life narratives. Axiologically, narrative therapy values respect for subjectivity, empowerment, and cultural sensitivity. It honours clients' worldviews, promotes self-determination, and decentralises the therapist's authority. Rather than imposing external frameworks, it supports clients in crafting narratives aligned with their values, goals, and cultural or spiritual beliefs. This approach upholds the dignity of diverse stories and encourages challenging dominant, limiting narratives imposed by external forces. Together, these epistemological, ontological, and axiological foundations create a therapeutic model that prioritises personal meaning-making, recognises culture and language in shaping experience, and empowers clients to reclaim authorship of their lives. Through externalisation and co-construction of preferred narratives, clients are guided to reshape their identities in ways reflecting their values and aspirations.

Islāmic epistemology is founded on an integrated view of knowledge, where revelation (*wahy*), reason (*'aql*), and empirical observation (*tajriba*) harmoniously coexist under the guidance of divine truth. Unlike secular frameworks that treat reason and sensory data as autonomous and value-neutral, Islāmic epistemology insists that all knowledge be interpreted through the lens of faith. Revelation, primarily through the Qur'ān and Sunnah, holds supreme authority and forms the foundation against which all other knowledge is measured. Reason and empirical experience are valued and encouraged, but their legitimacy depends on alignment with the absolute truths of divine revelation. Revelation thus acts not as a barrier to inquiry but as its moral and metaphysical anchor, ensuring that knowledge serves a higher spiritual purpose. This approach sharply contrasts with many contemporary psychological models grounded in secular, materialist assumptions, which often reduce humans to biological or cognitive systems influenced solely by environmental factors, neural activity, or unconscious drives.

In contrast, Islāmic thought views the human being as a multidimensional creation comprising *nafs* (self), *qalb* (heart), *'aql* (intellect), and *rūḥ* (spirit), all oriented towards a moral and spiritual purpose. Knowledge, therefore, transcends mere problem-solving or information gathering; it is a sacred pursuit aimed at aligning the self with the will of Allāh and fulfilling the ultimate purpose of existence, worshipping and knowing Him. Islām rejects both epistemological relativism and rigid objectivism. While relativism claims all perspectives are equally valid and truth is subjective, Islām asserts absolute moral and spiritual truths, such as the oneness of God and the sanctity of justice, which are non-negotiable. Conversely, Islām challenges rigid objectivism that limits knowledge to material or observable facts, excluding revelation and moral reasoning. For example, neuroscience might explain brain activity during prayer but cannot capture or replace the spiritual essence and divine purpose of that act. Islām offers a balanced epistemology, rooted in revelation, guided by reason, and open to empirical observation, all directed towards a truth that brings one closer to Allāh. This epistemological framework deeply impacts Muslim clients and therapists, especially in psychotherapy and counselling. Therapeutic approaches must go beyond mere tolerance of faith; they must meaningfully integrate Islāmic values and spiritual practices. For Muslims, faith is not peripheral or optional but central to identity and worldview.

Islāmic ontology views human existence as holistic and interconnected, where the spiritual, emotional, and physical dimensions are inseparable. Psychological well-being, therefore, extends beyond emotional regulation or behavioural change to include spiritual alignment and living according to one's divine purpose. Mental distress is not merely a biological or socio-environmental issue but may stem from spiritual disconnection or deviation from Islāmic values. This holistic outlook informs how Muslims understand suffering, healing, and human potential. In Islāmic psychotherapy, reality is not seen as subjective or relative but as grounded in divine truth. Central to this ontology is the concept of fitrah, the innate nature or disposition bestowed by Allāh. The Qur'ān affirms that every person is born with an inherent awareness of truth and a natural belief in God. Humans possess an intuitive grasp of moral goodness and are naturally inclined to submit to the One God. At its core, fitrah embodies the human tendency to love God, truth, and beauty. Rather than a blank slate (tabula rasa), humans begin life with an innate moral compass (Rassool, 2023, p. 98). It is narrated by Abu Hurayrah that Allāh's Messenger (ﷺ) said, "Every child is born with a true faith of Islām (i.e., to worship none but Allāh Alone) but his parents convert him to Judaism,

Christianity, or Magainism, as an animal delivers a perfect baby animal. Do you find it mutilated?" (Bukhârî). Allāh's Messenger (ﷺ) informed us that every child is born on the *fitrah*; this means that the child submits to the laws of Allāh as his Lord and Creator, and his soul adheres to the correct beliefs and truth. It is through his parents and the socialisation process that make him follow the religion of the parent or significant others (Rassool, 2023). This ontological perspective asserts that while external factors such as culture and society can influence a person, the core of their nature remains inclined towards righteousness and truth. It is through the preservation or corruption of *fitrah* that an individual's spiritual journey unfolds, making it central to Islāmic concepts of human nature and development.

Closely linked to this is Islāmic axiology, the moral and ethical framework derived from the Qur'ān, Sunnah, and Islamic tradition, that defines true psychological health. Wellness is seen as a state of inner peace, moral integrity, and spiritual harmony, not merely the absence of illness. Core values such as *tawḥīd* (oneness of God), *sabr* (patience), *shukr* (gratitude), *tawakkul* (trust in God), *'adl* (justice), *akhlāq* (moral character), and *rahmah* (mercy) guide Muslims in understanding and navigating psychological challenges. Islāmic ontology rests on the belief that reality is objective, created by Allāh, and governed by divine will. Reality is not a subjective human construct but exists independently of individual perception. One of Allāh's names is *Al-Haqq* (The Absolute Truth), affirming that ultimate reality is determined by His wisdom and decree (*qadar*). In this worldview, material and metaphysical realms are intertwined, and humans are created with the ultimate purpose of worshipping Allāh and living according to His guidance. The meaning of life in Islāmic thought centres on submission to Allāh and aligning with His divine plan. Humans find purpose through devotion, obedience, and fulfilling divine responsibilities. Living in accordance with God's guidance brings spiritual fulfillment and harmony with the natural and moral order established by Allāh. As the Qur'ān states

وَمَا خَلَقْتُ ٱلْجِنَّ وَٱلْإِنسَ إِلَّا لِيَعْبُدُونِ

- *I did not create jinn and humans except to worship Me* (Adh-Dhariyat 51:56, interpretation of the meaning).

Human experiences, including suffering and hardship, are not random or self-created but part of a greater divine purpose. While humans possess free will and self-determination, their existence remains inherently linked to the divine order. Thus, psychological healing extends beyond rewriting personal narratives; it involves aligning one's understanding with the ultimate truth revealed by Allāh. The laws of Allāh and the Sunnah of Prophet Muhammad (ﷺ) serve as guiding principles governing the natural order and human existence. Humans live within this divinely ordained reality, with their purpose being submission (*Islām*) and alignment with Allāh's will. Unlike postmodern perspectives that emphasize subjective realities, Islāmic ontology asserts that the ultimate truth is governed by divine wisdom, and human understanding should strive to comprehend and live according to these eternal truths.

Divergence and convergence of narrative therapy with Islāmic beliefs

Narrative therapy, a postmodern therapeutic approach, originates from a secular framework and differs significantly from Islāmic traditions in its epistemology, ontology, and axiology. However, its flexible and adaptable nature allows for the modification and integration of its techniques within the therapeutic process. The degree of alignment between narrative therapy and Islāmic principles depends on how its techniques are adapted to align with Islāmic teachings. While there are areas where the two can complement each other, certain assumptions and practices in narrative therapy may not be congruent with Islāmic beliefs.

One significant area of tension between narrative therapy and Islāmic principles lies in their treatment of spirituality and religious practices. Spirituality is not inherently integrated into the therapeutic process; instead, it is considered only if the client personally values it and brings it into the discussion. This aligns with narrative therapy's emphasis on valuing the client's autonomy and meaning-making, recognising them as the primary author of their life journey. As a result, religious or spiritual beliefs are treated as one possible lens among many rather than an essential foundation for healing. Western psychological frameworks often distinguish between spirituality and religiosity, with spirituality being seen as an individualised experience that may or may not involve religious affiliation, while religion is often associated with organised institutions and prescribed doctrines (Rassool, 2025a). This distinction reflects a broader cultural tendency in Western societies, where personal spiritual beliefs are often prioritised over institutionalised religious practices. Referring to White's (2000) definition of spirituality, he stated that

> When I talk of spirituality I am not appealing to the Divine or the holy. And I am not saluting human nature, whatever that might be, if it exists at all. The notion of spirituality that I am relating to is one that makes it possible for me to see and to appreciate the visible in people's lives, not the invisible... it is a spirituality that has to do with relating to one's material options in a way that one becomes more conscious of one's own knowing.
> (cited in McVeigh, 2016, p. 132)

White's idea of spirituality focuses on personal awareness and the visible aspects of life, rather than the Divine or the sacred. The approach of integrated spirituality in narrative therapy can be summarised as follows: Narrative therapy incorporates spirituality within its framework, viewing it as a means of fostering meaning and purpose in individuals' lives and extending this significance to their interpersonal relationships (Béres, 2014). This fits well within narrative therapy, which helps people make sense of their experiences through their own stories. The fragile relationship between postmodernism and spirituality, let alone religious value, may contribute to a sense of "spiritual groundlessness and yearning for connection" (Moules, 2000, p. 233). While some therapists practicing narrative therapy may incorporate spirituality when working with religious clients, the approach does not inherently recognise spiritual or divine dimensions of human experience. Instead, it prioritises deconstructing dominant narratives and reconstructing alternative, empowering stories based on the client's perspective, regardless of religious or metaphysical considerations.

In contrast, Islām considers spirituality and religious practices to be central to personal well-being and healing. Islāmic traditions do not separate spirituality from religion; they view both as deeply interconnected and essential to a Muslim's life. In Islām, spirituality (*ruḥāniyyah*) is inherently tied to religious doctrine, rituals, and moral conduct, all of which are guided by divine revelation. Islāmic teachings emphasise that psychological and emotional struggles are deeply connected to one's spiritual state. Healing is not merely a psychological reconstruction of personal narratives but a process that involves acts of worship, such as prayer (*ṣalāh*), fasting (*ṣawm*), charity (*sadaqah*), and remembrance of Allāh (*dhikr*). These acts are not just personal expressions of spirituality but also obligatory practices that shape a believer's relationship with the Divine (Rassool, 2025a). In summary, Islām sees spirituality as fundamental, while narrative therapy treats it as a personal choice. This distinction highlights that while narrative therapy can be beneficial, it may not fully address the spiritual needs of Muslim clients unless it incorporates their faith and beliefs.

Narrative therapy is rooted in postmodernism, which upholds pluralism and moral relativism. That is the idea that there is no single objective reality but multiple, equally valid perspectives on truth. From this perspective, no single worldview is considered superior, and all beliefs are treated as equally valid interpretations of reality. This aligns with the postmodern rejection of grand narratives or universal truths, emphasising personal meaning-making over adherence to any fixed belief system. The worldview underlying narrative therapy is fundamentally secular and postmodern (White & Epston, 1990). aligns with a secular worldview that separates knowledge from divine or metaphysical sources. This secular, human-centred worldview contrasts sharply with religious worldviews, particularly the Islāmic paradigm, where reality is not merely a human construct but rooted in divine truth. Al-Attas (2001) emphasises that in Islām, worldview is not merely a subjective or culturally conditioned perception of reality; rather, it constitutes a vision of reality and truth (*Ru'yat al-Islām li al-wujud*). This worldview encompasses both the temporal world (*dunyā*) and the eternal hereafter (*ākhirah*), creating a dual perspective that fundamentally shapes how Muslims interpret experiences and construct meaning. Consequently, therapeutic approaches that do not acknowledge this duality may struggle to resonate with Muslim clients or risk reinforcing existential conflicts. The Islāmic worldview is deeply rooted in the six core beliefs including: Belief in the Oneness of God (*tawḥīd*); Belief in the existence of angels (*malaikah*); Belief in divine scriptures (*kutub*); Belief in the prophets *(nubuwwah)*; Belief in the Day of Judgement and the afterlife (*akhirah*); and Belief in divine predestination (*qadr*). Together, these beliefs offer a holistic worldview that integrates faith, morality, and personal responsibility, providing a strong foundation for psychological and spiritual resilience, and ethical decision-making. The client's experiential worldview, central to narrative therapy's framing system, can be understood as a "story within a story" (Palmer, 2002). This highlights the importance of recognising the client's unique lens, which is shaped by religious, social, cultural, political, and historical influences. For Muslim clients, this lens is inherently informed by Islāmic teachings, which provide a comprehensive framework for understanding life, suffering, healing, and purpose. Therapeutic success depends on alignment with the client's worldview (Blow et al., 2012), and interventions that do not consider the Islāmic paradigm of reality may lead to existential conflicts.

A key area of divergence between Islāmic and secular worldviews lies in their perspectives on family interdependence versus individualism. Western psychological models, particularly those rooted in postmodern thought, centre on self-determination and autonomy, often considering family involvement secondary unless explicitly prioritised by the client. This approach assumes that psychological healing is primarily an internal process, where the individual must navigate their emotions, trauma, and identity independently. Hayward (2019) notes, that narrative therapy, like other systemic therapies, "does not so much privilege family relationships as significant relationships" (p. 7), focusing more on the individual's personal story than on the family as a collective entity. This focus on individual psychology, as pointed out by Minuchin (1998), can lead to the marginalisation of the family, potentially alienating them as a source of emotional and social support. In contrast, this individualistic focus may result in neglecting the impact that personal narratives have on familial relationships, potentially leading to conflicts within the family dynamic. For Muslim clients, this approach can be problematic, as it overlooks the vital role of the family in Islāmic teachings, which emphasise the family as a cornerstone of support, unity, and spiritual growth. It is narrated by Abu'l-'Anbas, who said, "I visited 'Abdullah ibn 'Amr at al-Waht (some land of his in Ta'if). He said, 'The Prophet (ﷺ), pointed his finger towards us and said, "Kinship *(Rahim)* is derived from the All-Merciful (*Rahman*). When someone maintains the connections of ties of kinship, they maintain connection with him. If someone cuts them off, they cut him off. They will have an unfettered, eloquent tongue on the Day of Rising."

(Al-Adab Al-Mufrad). Islāmic principles stress the central role of the family in a person's well-being, with the family considered a sacred institution and a continuous source of support, guidance, and connection to the broader community (Sabry & Vohra, 2013). While Islām acknowledges the need for healthy boundaries, it discourages estrangement and excessive individualism, promoting balance through mutual rights and responsibilities within the family structure. By disregarding the interconnectedness of the client's personal narrative with their family, narrative therapy may fall short in addressing the holistic needs of Muslim clients, who view their family as integral to their healing and spiritual journey.

In secular therapeutic models like narrative therapy, the emphasis is often on subjective meaning and the client's personal experience, rather than on objective or absolute truths. This perspective aligns with existential and humanistic psychology, which places the individual at the centre of meaning-making, suggesting that purpose is derived from personal choices, aspirations, and relationships. While this approach allows for flexibility, autonomy, and self-determination, it also leaves individuals vulnerable to existential crises, particularly in times of suffering or uncertainty when self-constructed meanings may collapse under emotional distress. In contrast, Islām provides an absolute and divinely ordained framework for meaning and purpose, rooted in submission to Allāh (*'ubūdiyyah*) and fulfilling one's role as His servant (*'abd*). The Qur'ân explicitly states that "I did not create jinn and humans except to worship Me" (Adh-Dhariyat 51:56, interpretation of the meaning). This verse establishes worship (*'ibādah*) as the fundamental purpose of human existence, encompassing not only ritual acts but also ethical living, service to others, and personal development in accordance with divine guidance. Islām offers a transcendent source of meaning, ensuring that even suffering and hardship have a higher purpose, whether as a test, a means of purification, or a path to spiritual growth. Unlike secular models, which rely on personal interpretation, Islām provides a stable and unchanging moral compass, offering clarity in navigating life's challenges. Thus, while secular psychology seeks meaning in self-defined narratives, Islām integrates meaning within a greater divine reality, fostering resilience, contentment, and a sense of ultimate accountability.

In narrative therapy, personal agency (an individual's ability to make choices, take control of their life, and shape their own narrative) is central to psychological well-being. Individuals are seen as the authors of their own stories, with the capacity to reinterpret past experiences, change their perspectives, and construct new stories that empower them. This emphasis on self-determination and autonomy aligns with the broader secular worldview, which prioritises human control over destiny. In this framework, meaning and change come from within the individual, and healing occurs through the re-authoring of one's life story. Narrative therapy emphasises the value of individual autonomy, where clients are seen as authors of their own stories, responsible for their actions, and capable of creating change in their lives. This perspective suggests that individuals have significant control over their decisions and circumstances. This approach can be empowering, as it enables individuals to break free from limiting beliefs and external influences, fostering a sense of ownership over their lives. However, this model largely excludes the role of divine intervention, which is a fundamental aspect of the Islāmic worldview. Islām, while acknowledging human free will *(ikhtiyār)*, emphasises that all actions ultimately unfold within the bounds of Divine will and decree (*al-Qadaa' wa'l-Qadar*). Allāh says in the Qur'ân:

وَمَا تَشَاؤُونَ إِلَّا أَن يَشَاءَ ٱللَّهُ ۚ إِنَّ ٱللَّهَ كَانَ عَلِيمًا حَكِيمًا

- *And you do not will except that Allāh wills. Indeed, Allāh is ever Knowing and Wise* (Al-Insan 76:30, interpretation of the meaning).

This means that while individuals are responsible for their choices and actions, they must also recognise the limitations of human control and place trust in Allāh's plan (*tawakkul*). Islāmic teachings affirm human free will and accountability for actions but emphasise the ultimate limits of self-determination, as all decisions are ultimately subject to Divine will and decree. This contrast highlights a fundamental tension between the narrative therapy concept of self-determination and the Islāmic belief in the decisive influence of Divine will and decree on human actions. Allāh says in the Qur'ân:

قُل لَّن يُصِيبَنَآ إِلَّا مَا كَتَبَ ٱللَّهُ لَنَا هُوَ مَوْلَىٰنَا ۚ وَعَلَى ٱللَّهِ فَلْيَتَوَكَّلِ ٱلْمُؤْمِنُونَ

- *Say, "Never will we be struck except by what God has decreed for us; He is our protector." And upon God let the believers rely.* (At-Tawbah 9:51, interpretation of the meaning).

In Islāmic psychotherapy, individual autonomy and Divine will and decree can coexist by integrating the client's beliefs and values with Islāmic principles in the therapeutic process. An Islāmic psychotherapist must strike a balance between acknowledging human agency and recognising the necessity of surrendering to Allāh's plan. This involves understanding the extent of personal control over actions while embracing the deeper connection between individual choices and Allāh's greater design. Central to this approach is seeking Allāh's guidance and cultivating complete trust and reliance (*tawakkul*) in Him.

In narrative therapy, suffering is often seen as a socially constructed experience that can be transformed through the re-authoring of one's story. Clients are encouraged to reinterpret their pain and challenges, seeing them as external to their identity, often framed as negative events that can be overcome through new narratives and perspectives. By shifting the way clients perceive and tell their stories, narrative therapy aims to empower individuals to gain control over their suffering, turning it into an opportunity for growth and healing. This perspective focuses on human agency, where the individual becomes the narrator who can reshape their experience of suffering into a meaningful, empowering story. While this can be a therapeutic tool, it may overlook the deeper spiritual dimensions of suffering, especially in cultures and religions where suffering is viewed as inherently meaningful. In contrast, Islām provides a spiritual framework for understanding suffering, emphasising that it is not merely a social construct but a test from Allāh and an opportunity for spiritual purification and growth. Trials, tribulations, and suffering should be endured with patience, as part of Allāh 's divine plan. In Islām, suffering is viewed as a means of spiritual refinement and an opportunity to strengthen faith. It can serve as a test of a person's trust in Allāh (*tawakkul)* and submission to His will. Rather than seeing suffering as something to be eliminated or avoided, Islām teaches that it is a natural part of life that leads to personal and spiritual growth. Healing, therefore, is not solely about changing one's narrative but about embracing suffering as a way to draw closer to Allāh, fostering resilience, gratitude, and humility that can lead to both personal transformation and a deeper connection to God.

In narrative therapy, change is primarily viewed as self-directed, with individuals actively reinterpreting and reframing their life events. The process focuses on empowerment through self-determination, encouraging clients to take control of their stories and redefine their past experiences in a way that supports personal growth and healing. This approach prioritises personal empowerment but may sometimes overlook the spiritual aspects of healing, particularly in contexts where divine guidance and intervention are integral. Islām, while also recognising the importance of personal effort and agency, integrates faith and divine intervention into the process of healing and change. In this framework, change is achieved not only through self-effort but also through reliance on faith (*īmān*), prayer (*salat*), and total reliance on Allāh (*tawakkul*). Islāmic healing acknowledges the importance of individual action in seeking improvement, whether through self-discipline, moral striving, or seeking knowledge. However, it is combined with a deep awareness that true transformation is ultimately subject to Allāh's will and divine decree (*qadar*). This highlights a convergence with narrative therapy in the sense that both approaches value personal agency. However, Islām places a stronger emphasis on the role of divine guidance and trust in Allah's plan. Thus, healing in Islām is a harmonious blend of self-effort and divine assistance, grounded in spiritual practices and reliance on God's mercy and wisdom.

Narrative therapy emphasises externalising problems, a process where clients are encouraged to see their issues as separate from their identity. This technique helps individuals' distance themselves from their difficulties, allowing them to reinterpret life events and recast their problems in a way that fosters empowerment and change. By rewriting personal narratives, clients can reframe negative experiences, reducing feelings of shame or blame. This approach highlights the importance of cognitive restructuring, transforming the way a person understands and interacts with their struggles. The therapeutic focus is on reshaping the individual's relationship with their challenges, offering a pathway to personal growth through new perspectives and greater control over one's narrative. Islāmic psychotherapy, in contrast, does not focus solely on externalising problems but encourages clients to integrate their spiritual and faith-based practices into the healing process. Reliance on faith, coupled with prayer (*salat*), supplication (*du'ah*), reciting the Qur'ân, and seeking divine guidance (*istikhara*), is central to the Islāmic approach. While Islāmic therapy recognises the importance of self-reflection and personal effort in overcoming difficulties, it deeply roots healing within a spiritual context, where problems are often seen as tests from Allāh meant to purify and strengthen faith. In this approach, individuals are encouraged to rely on trust in Allāh, acknowledging that ultimate transformation and relief from suffering come through divine intervention. While both narrative therapy and Islāmic psychotherapy encourage reinterpretation of life experiences, the key divergence is that Islāmic psychotherapy integrates spiritual interventions at every step of the healing journey.

A summary of the areas of congruence and tension between narrative therapy and the Islāmic worldview/Islāmic psychotherapy is presented in Table 3.1.

Table 3.1 A summary of the areas of congruence and tension between narrative therapy and the Islāmic worldview/Islāmic psychotherapy

Aspect	Narrative therapy	Islāmic worldview / Islāmic psychotherapy	Congruence / tension
View of reality	Reality is socially and linguistically constructed; multiple truths exist.	Reality is ultimately objective and grounded in divine revelation (Qur'ân and Sunnah).	Tension: Islām affirms an absolute truth, while narrative therapy emphasises subjective truths.
Human nature	People are seen as meaning-makers, shaped by personal and social narratives.	Humans are created with *fitrah* (natural disposition) and moral accountability.	Congruence: Both value human meaning-making and growth, but differ in their view of ultimate reality.
Change process	Clients re-author their stories to align with preferred identities and values.	Change involves spiritual, psychological, and moral realignment with divine guidance.	Partial congruence: Both seek transformation, but Islām roots it in alignment with God's will.

(Continued)

Table 3.1 Continued

Aspect	Narrative therapy	Islāmic worldview / Islāmic psychotherapy	Congruence / tension
Therapist's role	Collaborative, non-expert stance; helps client explore alternative narratives.	Therapist is a guide (sometimes also spiritual), integrating faith and therapy.	Congruence: Emphasis on empathy and collaboration aligns well, though Islāmic therapists may also act as moral guides.
Language and meaning	Language constructs identity and shapes reality.	Language is powerful but ultimately subordinate to divine truth and scripture.	Partial tension: Islām values language highly (e.g., Qur'ān), but not as a constructor of reality itself.
Values and ethics	Non-directive, values are client-defined.	Ethical values are rooted in divine commandments and Prophetic tradition.	Tension: In Islām, ethics are not fully relative or client-defined.
View of suffering	Problems are separate from the person and constructed through stories and context.	Suffering has meaning (e.g., test, purification) and is part of divine decree.	Congruence: Both offer non-pathologising views of suffering, though Islām adds theological depth.
Identity and self	Identity is fluid, multi-storied, and co-constructed.	Identity is defined by one's relationship with Allah, community, and spiritual purpose.	Tension: Islām provides a fixed, God-centred foundation for identity.
Hope and empowerment	Empowerment through re-authoring and agency in meaning-making.	Empowerment through *tawakkul* (trust in God), *du'ā'h*, and spiritual striving.	Partial congruence: Both promote empowerment, though sources differ.

Conclusion

Narrative therapy can be a valuable tool for an Islāmic psychotherapist working with Muslim clients, provided there is alignment between the Islāmic worldview and the approach's underlying philosophical foundations. Narrative therapy offers a flexible framework that can, in many cases, be adapted to Islāmic values. In this context, the Qur'ān and *Sunnah* become integral components of the therapeutic process, aiding Muslim clients in deriving meaning and purpose in their lives. The externalisation of problems in narrative therapy can also be adapted. Islām teaches that not all challenges stem purely from within. The Qur'ān and *Sunnah* often highlight the external forces, like societal pressures or harmful environments, that can affect human behaviour. For example, *Shaytan* (Satan) is described as a deceiver who influences human actions, and believers are encouraged to be vigilant against such influences (Al 'Araf 7:200). Additionally, the concept of externalising problems in narrative therapy needs to be handled thoughtfully, as some aspects of Islāmic psychology suggest that individuals should view their struggles as part of their test from Allah, not as external entities to be separated from the self.

Storytelling is a powerful tool in both the Qur'ān and *hadīth*, used not only to convey moral lessons but also to guide individuals in navigating life's challenges. These narratives are not mere accounts of events but serve as spiritual and psychological lessons, offering insight into coping with adversity, maintaining faith, and understanding the divine plan. By integrating these stories into an Islāmic integrated narrative therapy, therapists can guide Muslim clients to reframe their personal struggles within the context of these sacred narratives. Spiritual interventions, including remembrance of Allah (*dhikr*), supplication (*du'ah*), and prayer (*salah*) can complement the narrative reframing process. While there is a dissonance between narrative therapy and the Islāmic worldview, particularly regarding the social construction of knowledge and reality, Islāmic psychotherapists can still effectively utilise narrative therapy by understanding its underlying philosophical assumptions. This understanding enables them to "sanctify" the discipline, making it more reflective of how God continues to be the healing force in all healing arts (Hankle, 2016, p. 13). Hankle's observation is particularly relevant to the Islāmic worldview. By recognising these philosophical foundations, Islāmic therapists can integrate narrative therapy in a manner that aligns with Islāmic principles, placing emphasis on the role of God as the ultimate source of healing.

References

Al-Adab Al-Mufrad 54. *In-book reference: Book 2,* Hadith 8. English translation: Book 2, Hadith 54. Sahih (Al-Albani). https://sunnah.com/adab/2.

Al-Attas, M. N. (2001). *Prolegomena to the metaphysics of Islām: An exposition of the fundamental elements of the worldview of Islām* (pp. 252–256). ISTAC.

Béres, L. (2014). *The narrative practitioner.* Macmillan International Higher Education.

Blow, A. J., Davis, S. D., & Sprenkle, D. H. (2012). Therapist-worldview matching: Not as important as matching to clients. *Journal of Marital and Family Therapy,* *38*(1s), 13–17.

Bukhârî. *Sahih al-Bukhari 1385.* In-book reference: Book 23, Hadith 137. USC-MSA web (English) reference: Vol. 2, Book 23, Hadith 467. https://sunnah.com/bukhari:1385.

Hankle, D. D. (2016). Christian worldview and the use of narrative therapy in the Christian counseling setting. *Journal of Christian Healing, 32*(1), 5–24.

Hayward, M. (2019). *Critiques of narrative therapy: A personal response.* https://theint.co.uk/wp-content/uploads/2019/02/critiques-of-narrative-therapy-a-personal-response.pdf

McVeigh, A. K. (2016). Spirituality in practice: An exploration into narrative practitioners' approaches to addressing spirituality in counselling practices [Unpublished master's thesis, Unitec Institute of Technology]. https://hdl.handle.net/10652/3285

Minuchin, P. (1988). Relationships within the family: A systems perspective on development. In R. A. Hinde & J. Stevenson-Hinde (Eds.), *Relationships within families: Mutual influences* (pp. 7–25). Clarendon Press.

Minuchin, P., Colapinto, J., & Salvador, M. (1998). *Working with families of the poor.* Guilford Press.

Minuchin, S., & Nichols, M. P. (1998). Structural family therapy. In F. M. Dattilio (Ed.), *Case studies in couple and family therapy: Systemic and cognitive perspectives* (pp. 108–131). The Guilford Press.

Moules, N. (2000). Postmodernism and the sacred: Reclaiming connection in our greater-than-human worlds. *Journal of Marital and Family Therapy, 26*(2), 229–240. https://doi.org/10.1111/j.1752-0606.2000.tb00292.x.

Palmer, M. D. (2002). *Elements of a Christian worldview.* Logion Press.

Rassool, G. Hussein. (2023). *Islāmic psychology: The basics.* Routledge.

Rassool, G. Hussein. (2025a). *Islāmic counselling & psychotherapy: From theory to practice* (2nd ed.). Routledge.

Rassool, G. Hussein. (2025b). *Exploring the intersection of Islāmic spiritual and psychotherapy: Healing the soul.* Springer.

Rassool, G. Hussein. (2025c). *Spiritual integration in Islāmic psychotherapy: Unveiling the therapist's soul.* Focus Series on Islāmic Psychology & Psychotherapy. Routledge.

Sabry, W. M., & Vohra, A. (2013). Role of Islām in the management of psychiatric disorders. *Indian Journal of Psychiatry, 55*(Suppl 2), S205–S214.

White, M., & Epston, D. (1990). *Narrative means to therapeutic ends.* WW.Norton & Company.

Willig, C. (2019). Ontological and epistemological reflexivity: A core skill for therapists. *Counselling and Psychotherapy Research, 19*(3), 186–194.

4 Unveiling an Islāmic Integrated Narrative Therapy model

Introduction

Islāmic Integrated Narrative Therapy (IINT) blends narrative therapy with Islāmic teachings, offering a spiritually grounded approach to psychological healing. Unlike traditional narrative therapy, which focuses primarily on personal empowerment and self-authorship, IINT situates the process within the framework of Islāmic principles, particularly submission to Allāh's will and the pursuit of His pleasure. Clients are encouraged to reconstruct their life stories in alignment with Qur'ānic values and prophetic teachings, balancing self-determination with acceptance of *qadar* (divine decree) and a focus on spiritual growth. This model provides a holistic path to healing by integrating emotional and psychological development with spiritual well-being. It empowers individuals to take back control of their life stories while staying rooted in faith, guided by Allāh, and supported by their community and family. This chapter introduces the core elements of IINT, including *tawhīd*, divine will, personal narrative reframing, and collective healing.

Components of the Islāmic integrated narrative therapy model

The IINT model integrates several key components that foster holistic healing. At its core are the Tawhîd paradigm, the Divine Will (*tawakkul & qadar*), which grounds the therapeutic process in submission to Allāh's wisdom. The model emphasises the importance of the client's narrative, allowing individuals to reshape their self-perception and life story through therapeutic reframing. Islāmic storytelling, using the Qur'ān and *hadīth*, provides guiding narratives for healing, while metaphors from Islāmic teachings facilitate deeper emotional transformation. Spiritual interventions enhance the process, and community and family support play a vital role in collective healing, creating a comprehensive approach that nurtures emotional, mental, and spiritual well-being. Figure 4.1 presents the model of Islāmic modified narrative therapy.

DOI: 10.4324/9781003584995-5

Figure 4.1 Islāmic Integrated Narrative Therapy.

Tawhîd paradigm

At the core of the IINT Model is the *Tawhîd* paradigm, a holistic framework in Islāmic psychotherapy grounded in the belief in the oneness of God. This paradigm affirms Allāh as the sole Creator, Sustainer, and ultimate Healer. The foundational principles of this paradigm have been explored in depth elsewhere (Rassool, 2024a), highlighting key components such as *Tawhîd, fitrah, taqwa* (God-consciousness), the Islāmic worldview, holistic and spiritual integration, balance, spiritual motivation, and ethical intelligence (Rassool, 2024b, p. 22).

These principles have since been refined and synthesised into a new Islāmic framework. Within this updated framework, monotheism (*Tawhîd*) is seen as intrinsically linked to the human *fitrah,* the natural disposition to acknowledge and worship one God. From this foundation arises faith (*Imān*), which nurtures God-consciousness (*Taqwa*), inspires spiritual motivation, encourages sincere worship (*Ibadat*), and fosters the growth of ethical intelligence. These dimensions collectively shape character and guide behaviour in accordance with divine guidance. The broader Islāmic worldview expands on this by affirming theism (*Tawhîd*), humanity's role as vicegerent (*Khilâfah*),

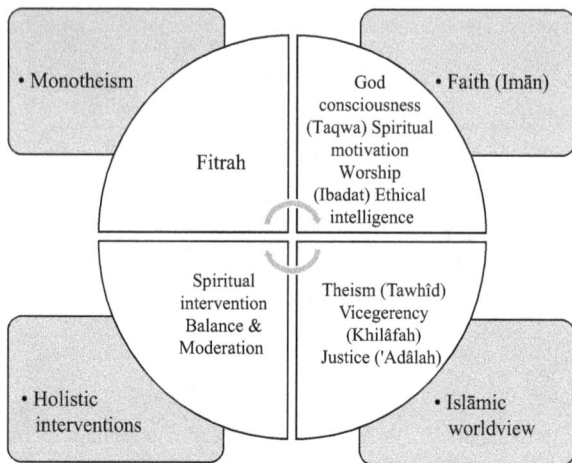

Figure 4.2 The Elements of the Tawhîd Paradigm.

and the pursuit of justice (*'Adâlah*). Therapeutically, this perspective promotes holistic interventions that integrate spirituality and encourages balance and moderation in mental, emotional, and social well-being, providing a truly comprehensive and faith-aligned path to healing. Figure 4.2 presents the elements of the *Tawhîd* paradigm.

Tawhîd is the fundamental Islāmic belief in the Oneness of Allāh. This principle not only affirms Allāh as the Creator of all things but also highlights that everything in existence operates under His divine control and wisdom. This unicity of God is "the very foundation of Islām on which all the other pillars and principles depend. If one's *Tawhîd* is not sound, the rest of one's Islām becomes, in effect, a series of pagan rituals. In this model, Allāh's unity must be maintained"(Phillips, 1994, p. vii). The *Tawhîd* paradigm in Islāmic psychotherapy is a holistic approach rooted in the principle of *Tawhîd,* which affirms the oneness of God as the sole creator, sustainer, and ruler of the universe (Rassool, 2024a). This paradigm views

> All aspects of life, including mental health, are interconnected and should be understood within the framework of *Tawhîd,* emphasising unity and coherence in a person's spiritual, psychological, and social life. The oneness of God is central to understanding the human condition, meaning and purpose. It recognises that human beings are interconnected with God, and that a balanced and healthy relationship with God is essential for psychological health and purification of the soul.
>
> (Rassool, 2024a, p. 22)

Thus, accepting the belief that true healing and well-being ultimately come from Him. The *Tawhîd* paradigm in Islāmic psychotherapy is a holistic framework that integrates spirituality, psychology, and ethics, emphasising the oneness of Allāh as the foundation of human well-being (Rassool, 2024b).

Tawhîd and *fitrah* are deeply interconnected in Islām. *Fitrah* refers to the natural, pure state every human is born with, an innate recognition of the existence and oneness of Allah. This inborn disposition inclines every person towards truth, morality, and the worship of one true Creator. *Tawhîd* is the core truth embedded in the *fitrah*. However, *fitrah* can become clouded or corrupted over time, by external influences such as societal influences, personal choices, environmental factors, culture, desires, or misguidance. The distortion of *fitrah* can lead to deviations from the innate inclination towards goodness and righteousness. The purpose of Islām, in many ways, is to restore and align the human self with its original state of *fitrah* through the clear understanding and practice of *Tawhîd*. Reconnecting with this innate monotheistic belief is also seen as essential to spiritual and psychological well-being in Islāmic thought.

Faith (*Imān*) is the foundation of a Muslim's spiritual and moral life. It is more than belief; it is a deep, inner conviction that connects the heart (*qalb*) to Allāh and shapes every aspect of one's behaviour and worldview. For faith to exist in Islām, it must meet all the criteria of the six axioms of the articles of faith (*Imān*) known as *Arkān al-īmān*: Belief in one God (*Tawhîd*); Belief in His Angels (*Malaikah*); Belief in His Books (*Kutub*); Belief in the Prophets (*Nubuwwah*); Belief in the Last Day and the Afterlife (*Akhirah*); and Belief in Predestination (*Al Qadr*). When faith is strong, it naturally gives rise to *taqwa*, which cannot exist without *Imān*. The concept of *taqwa* is often translated as "God-consciousness" or "piety," but its meaning is much deeper and more comprehensive. At the heart of *taqwa* is a constant awareness of Allāh's presence. It means being mindful of His knowledge, power, and mercy in every action and decision. It is the driving force behind a Muslim's ethical, spiritual, and behavioural conduct. This level of consciousness shapes how we interact with the world, reminding us to uphold honesty, justice, patience, and humility, even when no one is watching. From this faith and god-consciousness also emerges spiritual motivation, Spiritual motivation "is one aspect of motivation that focus on prioritising the moral good and implement ethical actions over other behavioural goals" (Rassool, 2021, p. 252). Spiritual motivation, deeply intertwined with *fitrah*, acts as an internal drive that compels individuals to seek meaning, purpose, and a connection with Allāh, forming the foundation of healing in Islāmic psychotherapy. The taxonomies of the spiritual model of motivation from an Islāmic perspective, which include intrinsic and extrinsic motivation, spiritual capital, and ethical intelligence, are examined in Rassool (2021).

Spiritual motivation leads to worship (*ibadat*), not just in rituals like prayer and fasting, but in all actions done for the sake of Allāh. Regular worship such as prayer (*salah*), fasting (*sawm*), *zakat*, and reading the Qur'ân reinforces *taqwa*. These acts are not mere rituals but spiritual practices that train the soul, purify the heart, and align the individual with divine will. Allāh says in the Qur'ân

يَـٰٓأَيُّهَا ٱلَّذِينَ ءَامَنُواْ كُتِبَ عَلَيْكُمُ ٱلصِّيَامُ كَمَا كُتِبَ عَلَى ٱلَّذِينَ مِن قَبْلِكُمْ لَعَلَّكُمْ تَتَّقُونَ

- *O you who have believed, decreed upon you is fasting as it was decreed upon those before you that you may become righteous.*(Al Baqarah 2:183, interpretation of the meaning)

Faith also fosters ethical intelligence. Ethical intelligence involves the ability to recognise, understand, and navigate moral and ethical issues effectively (Rassool, 2024c). It involves evaluating the moral consequences of actions, making ethical choices, and acting in alignment with ethical principles and values. Ethically intelligent psychotherapists not only understand what is right or wrong but also recognise when and how to act ethically in order to promote moral good. This extends beyond mere knowledge of ethical rules to include the ability and commitment to do what is morally right. This *Tawhîd* paradigm integrates Islāmic rules, theology, and spirituality to guide therapeutic practices, promoting goodness (*'amr bil ma'aruf*) and preventing what is wrong (*nahi al-munkar*).

The *Tawhîd* paradigm is established on an Islāmic worldview (*Tasawur or Ru'yah al-Islām li al-Wujud*) which is based on the Qur'ān and *Sunnah*, and the Islāmic civilisation. This means that worldview is a set of parameters that include a wide range of fundamental matters, including a philosophy, themes, values, emotions, ethics, language, culture, religion, and having a vision about, and interacting with our world. The Islāmic worldview is "based on three fundamental principles which are: *Tawhîd* (theism), *Khilâfah* (vicegerency), and *'Adâlah* (justice) (Al-Attas, 1995). These principles not only frame the Islāmic worldview, but they also constitute the fountainhead of the objectives. Holistic healing is central to *Tawhîd* paradigm in Islāmic psychotherapy, addressing the spiritual, psychological, and physical dimensions of an individual, integrating faith-based practices. Integrating faith and spirituality into therapy encourages clients to explore their beliefs, values, and spiritual practices as a source of meaning, purpose, and inner strength. This approach incorporates Islāmic teachings and spiritual interventions, including Qur'ānic verses, metaphor in the Qur'ān, Prophetic traditions, and stories of the Prophets to help individuals align their struggles with a greater spiritual perspective. Through this understanding, personal narratives are reframed within the context of faith in Allāh's divine plan (*qadar*), with healing and meaning derived from *tawakkul* (trust in Allāh) and divine wisdom (Rassool, 2024a). The principle of *wasatiyyah* (balance and moderation) is also essential, advocating for a measured, just, and harmonious approach to physical, social, mental, and spiritual well-being. Within the framework of IINT, the

Tawhîd paradigm offers a faith-centred, ethical, and integrative approach to mental health, guiding individuals towards spiritual fulfillment, resilience, and a deeper connection with Allāh.

Divine will (*tawakkul & qadar*)

At the heart of this model, in connection with the concept of *Tawhîd*, lies the element of Divine Will, embodied in *tawakkul* and *qadr*, which forms the foundation of the IINT. The principles of *tawakkul* (trust and reliance on Allāh) and *qadar* (divine decree) are essential in transforming personal narratives and building psychological resilience. *Tawakkul* involves placing complete trust in Allāh while simultaneously taking proactive steps to navigate and overcome life's difficulties. Allāh says in the Qur'ân:

وَمَن يَتَوَكَّلْ عَلَى ٱللَّهِ فَهُوَ حَسْبُهُۥ

- *And whoever relies upon Allāh–then He is sufficient for him. "* (At-Talaq 65:3, interpretation of the meaning)

Rather than surrendering to passive resignation, *Tawakkul* emphasises the importance of striving to fulfil one's responsibilities while simultaneously relying on God's guidance and wisdom for outcomes beyond human control. The Qur'ân emphasises this reliance:

قُل لَّن يُصِيبَنَآ إِلَّا مَا كَتَبَ ٱللَّهُ لَنَا هُوَ مَوْلَىٰنَا ۚ وَعَلَى ٱللَّهِ فَلْيَتَوَكَّلِ ٱلْمُؤْمِنُونَ

- *Say, "Never will we be struck except by what Allāh has decreed for us; He is our protector." And upon Allāh let the believers rely.* (At-Tawbah 9:51, interpretation of the meaning)

This verse teaches that, while we take the necessary steps in life, ultimately, everything happens according to Allāh's will. True reliance is the acknowledgement that no matter what happens, Allāh is the ultimate protector and sustainer, and He controls everything. Another powerful verse on reliance is

فَإِذَا عَزَمْتَ فَتَوَكَّلْ عَلَى ٱللَّهِ ۚ إِنَّ ٱللَّهَ يُحِبُّ ٱلْمُتَوَكِّلِينَ

- *And when you have decided, then rely upon Allāh. Indeed, Allāh loves those who rely [upon Him].* (Surah Al-Imran 3:159, interpretation of the meaning)

This perspective encourages believers to make decisions with confidence, then place complete trust in Allāh, assured that He will guide and support them through every outcome. *Tawakkul* encompasses both action and faith, putting in sincere effort while trusting in Allāh's plan and timing. In IINT, *tawakkul* holds a central role by shifting the focus from self-reliance to divine reliance, without diminishing personal responsibility. This approach does not promote passivity; rather, it cultivates a balanced approach that combines trust in Allāh with intentional effort. Through surrendering to divine wisdom, individuals can experience inner peace even amid hardship. The Islāmic view of adversity embraces both agency and submission, encouraging believers to actively pursue positive change while maintaining steadfast trust in Allāh's decree. In IINT, *tawakkul* functions as a spiritual coping strategy, allowing clients to release their fears and anxieties to Allāh while continuing to act responsibly and constructively.

Qadar (Divine Decree) is a fundamental concept in Islām and one of the Articles of Faith. Acceptance of divine will (*Rida bi'l-Qada*) is a core spiritual principle, and it refers to Allāh's predestination and divine wisdom in determining the course of events in the universe. A verse from the Qur'ân that addresses the concept of *qadar* (divine predestination) is found in Surah Al-Qamar:

$$إِنَّا كُلَّ شَىْءٍ خَلَقْنَـٰهُ بِقَدَرٍ$$

- *Indeed, all things We created with predestination.* (Al- Qamar 54:49, interpretation of the meaning)

This verse emphasises the belief that everything in the universe, from the smallest detail to the most significant event, unfolds according to Allāh's divine plan and predestination. It affirms that Allāh possesses complete knowledge and authority over all matters, and that nothing happens without His will and wisdom. Belief in *qadar* promotes acceptance of life's outcomes while acknowledging individual responsibility within the framework of divine decree. In IINT, *qadar* holds deep significance by encouraging individuals to interpret their life experiences through the lens of divine will. This perspective helps foster the understanding that both hardships and achievements are integral parts of Allāh's greater plan. IINT, by embedding these principles into the therapeutic process, encourages individuals to trust in Allāh's wisdom, accept the uncertainties of life, and actively participate in their own healing and growth.

Client's narrative (life story)

In IINT, the client's personal narrative is a core element of the therapeutic process. The approach is grounded in the understanding that the stories people construct about themselves shape their identity and influence their behaviour. These narratives are not static; they are fluid and open to being re-authored. A key technique in narrative therapy is "externalising" the problem, viewing the issue as separate from the individual which helps the client distinguish themselves from the problem, making it easier to work towards change and reshape their narrative. In IINT, the technique of externalising problems is enhanced with Islāmic spiritual principles to deepen client insight and facilitate meaningful transformation. This approach enables individuals to separate their struggles from their core identity, while simultaneously recognising these challenges as part of Allāh's divine will. Rather than merely creating distance from one's difficulties, IINT reframes them as opportunities for both spiritual and psychological growth, grounded in key concepts such as *tawakkul* and *qadar*. In many Muslim communities, emotional and psychological distress is often interpreted through spiritual or supernatural frameworks, such as the influence of *Jinn* (spiritual beings), the evil eye (*'ayn*), or possession (Rassool, 2019). These culturally and religiously rooted beliefs play a significant role in how individuals understand and respond to their experiences. For instance, a client experiencing panic attacks might say, "A *Jinn* is attacking me at night; I feel its presence and can't breathe." What distinguishes IINT from conventional narrative therapy is its integration of Islāmic teachings and faith-based reflection into the therapeutic process. While traditional narrative therapy focuses on externalising problems and re-authoring life stories for empowerment, IINT extends this approach by incorporating spiritual principles. By doing so, it helps clients interpret their struggles through a lens of divine purpose and spiritual growth.

Therapeutic reframing (new meaning-making)

Once the problem has been externalised, therapeutic reframing becomes a vital next step in the therapeutic process. This technique helps clients shift their perspective by introducing new ways of understanding their experiences and challenges. Reframing allows them to recognise that their struggles are shaped by external influences, such as social, cultural, and historical factors, rather than being inherent to their core self. In the IINT model, this reframing process is further enriched by an Islāmic worldview. After externalising the problem, clients are supported in interpreting their challenges through the lens of faith. They are encouraged to view these struggles not as permanent flaws or personal failings, but as tests (*fitnah*) from Allāh, temporary trials designed as part of their spiritual journey. From an Islāmic perspective, life's hardships are seen as opportunities to develop qualities such as patience (*sabr*), resilience, and deeper trust in Allāh. This faith-based reframing empowers clients to find meaning and purpose in their suffering, helping them grow both spiritually and emotionally.

In the Qur'ân, Allāh mentions that trials are inevitable, but they are also part of a divine plan designed to purify and strengthen believers. Allāh says in the Qur'ân:

وَٱلثَّمَرَٰتِ ۗ وَبَشِّرِ ٱلصَّٰبِرِينَ وَلَنَبْلُوَنَّكُم بِشَىْءٍ مِّنَ ٱلْخَوْفِ وَٱلْجُوعِ وَنَقْصٍ مِّنَ ٱلْأَمْوَٰلِ وَٱلْأَنفُسِ

- *And we will certainly test you with something of fear, hunger, loss of wealth, lives, and fruits. But give good tidings to the patient (Sabr).* (Al-Baqarah 2:155, interpretation of the meaning)

According to the exegesis of Ibn 'Abbâs, the verse refers to Allāh's trials upon the believers: "Then He mentioned His trial to the believer, saying: (And surely We shall try you), test you with fear of the enemy, hunger during times of drought, and the loss of wealth, lives, and crops through death, illness, or other hardships." Ibn Kathir further explains, "The believer is patient in the face of affliction and thus earns reward. Allāh informs us that He tests and tries His servants." This verse highlights that trials are an inevitable part of life, but they also serve as pathways for developing patience and perseverance, promoting both personal and spiritual growth. In Islam, core virtues such as patience (*ṣabr*), gratitude (*shukr*), belief in Divine Will (*qadar*), and reliance on Allāh *(tawakkul)* are essential in understanding and enduring life's hardships. Through therapeutic reframing in IINT, clients are guided to reinterpret their difficulties not as punishments, but as divinely ordained tests. These challenges are seen as opportunities for spiritual development and inner growth, encouraging a deeper sense of purpose and connection with Allāh.

Community & family support (collective healing)

IINT recognises the vital role of community and family in the healing journey. In contrast to Western individualistic models that often prioritise personal autonomy and self-responsibility in achieving well-being, Islāmic thought offers a more collective and interconnected approach to mental health. Healing, from an Islāmic perspective, is not viewed as the responsibility of the individual alone; rather, it is rooted in a network of supportive relationships, including family, close companions, and the wider Ummah (Muslim community). This collective approach is rooted in the Qur'ânic principle of mutual support and cooperation, as seen in the verse:

وَتَعَاوَنُواْ عَلَى ٱلْبِرِّ وَٱلتَّقْوَىٰ ۖ وَلَا تَعَاوَنُواْ عَلَى ٱلْإِثْمِ وَٱلْعُدْوَٰنِ ۚ

- *And cooperate in righteousness and piety, but do not cooperate in sin and aggression.* (Al Ma'idah 5:2, interpretation of the meaning)

In his exegesis, Ibn Kathir explains that this verse instructs believing servants to support one another in performing righteous and good deeds – referred to as *al-birr*, and to avoid sinful actions, which aligns with the concept of *taqwā*. Allāh prohibits believers from cooperating in sin (*ithm*) and transgression. Ibn Jarir further clarifies that *ithm* refers to neglecting what Allāh has commanded, while transgression involves exceeding the boundaries set by Allāh in matters of faith and conduct, both for oneself and others. This verse promotes a sense of communal responsibility, encouraging believers to unite in acts of goodness and mutual support. It highlights the importance of fostering a collective environment where emotional and spiritual well-being is nurtured through shared accountability and care. In this communal framework, healing is not seen as an isolated, individual pursuit, as often emphasised in the

Western individualistic model, but as a collective effort in which members of the community actively support one another's well-being. The concept of kinship, or *Silat al-rahim* (the ties of kinship), is central to Islāmic teachings, where maintaining strong, supportive relationships with family members is not only encouraged but also seen as a religious duty. Islāmic teachings place great importance on maintaining close and respectful relationships with family members. Allāh says in the Qur'ân:

$$لَّيْسَ ٱلْبِرَّ أَن تُوَلُّوا۟ وُجُوهَكُمْ قِبَلَ ٱلْمَشْرِقِ وَٱلْمَغْرِبِ وَلَٰكِنَّ ٱلْبِرَّ مَنْ ءَامَنَ بِٱللَّهِ وَٱلْيَوْمِ ٱلْءَاخِرِ وَٱلْمَلَٰٓئِكَةِ وَٱلْكِتَٰبِ وَٱلنَّبِيِّۦنَ وَءَاتَى ٱلْمَالَ عَلَىٰ حُبِّهِۦ ذَوِى ٱلْقُرْبَىٰ وَٱلْيَتَٰمَىٰ وَٱلْمَسَٰكِينَ وَٱبْنَ ٱلسَّبِيلِ وَٱلسَّآئِلِينَ$$

- *Righteousness is not that you turn your faces toward the east or the west, but [true] righteousness is [in] one who believes in Allāh, the Last Day, the angels, the Book, and the prophets and gives wealth, in spite of love for it, to relatives, orphans, the needy, the traveler, those who ask [for help]...* (Al-Baqarah 2:177, interpretation of the meaning)

In his exegesis, A'la Maududi stated that

It is no virtue. That you turn your faces towards the east or the west, but virtue is that one should sincerely believe in Allāh and the Last Day and the Angels and the Book and the Prophets and, out of His love, spend of one's choice wealth for relatives and orphans, for the needy and the wayfarer, for beggars.

It is narrated by Abu Hurairah that the Prophet (ﷺ) said, "Whoever believes in Allāh and the Last Day, should serve his guest generously; and whoever believes in Allāh and the Last Day, should unite the bond of kinship (i.e. keep good relation with his kith and kin). (Bukhârî). However, kinship ties extend beyond the immediate family to include a broader network of relatives, such as siblings, aunts, uncles, and cousins. Abu Ayyub al-Ansari told him that a Bedouin came to the Prophet (ﷺ), while he was travelling. He asked, "Tell me what will bring me near to the Garden and keep me far from the Fire." He replied, "Worship Allāh and do not associate anything with Him, perform the prayer, pay zakat, and maintain ties of kinship" (Al-Adab Al-Mufrad 49). Abu'l-'Anbas said, "I visited 'Abdullah ibn 'Amr at al-Waht (some land of his in Ta'if)." He said, "The Prophet (ﷺ) pointed his finger towards us and said, 'Kinship (rahim) us derived from the All-Merciful (Rahman). When someone maintains the connections of ties of kinship, they maintain connection with him. If someone cuts them off, they cut him off. They will have an unfettered, eloquent tongue on the Day of Rising' (Al-Adab Al-Mufrad 54). Moreover, family and relatives are more entitled to one's kind treatment than others, as pointed out by the Prophet's following hadīth. Abd Allāh bin 'Amr reported the Messenger of Allāh (ﷺ) as saying: "It is sufficient sin for a man that he neglects him whom he maintains." (Abū Dāwūd). The hadīth high-lights the serious responsibility of providing care and support to those under one's guardianship, particularly family members. This is a powerful reminder of the ethical duty in Islām to uphold family responsibilities. In summary, kin-ship in Islām extends beyond mere blood relations; it embodies broader soci-etal values such as mutual support, compassion, and shared responsibility. It reflects the Islāmic ideal of a cohesive and interconnected community, where each individual's well-being is upheld through collective care and coopera-tion. Central to this framework is the deep respect and honour given to one's parents, a foundational principle in Islāmic ethics.

There is substantial evidence indicating that Muslims often seek support from family, friends, and religious leaders before turning to professional ther-apy (Khan, 2014). Studies have shown that Muslim clients generally prefer to address personal and familial challenges within their close-knit communi-ties rather than pursuing external professional assistance. For example, Gra-ham et al. (2008) found that Muslim individuals typically rely on familial or community-based support systems before considering formal interventions. Similarly, Carolan et al. (2000) observed that American Muslims often seek advice from trusted family members or friends, particularly in the context of relationship issues, frequently turning to their spouse's family for guidance. Springer et al. (2009) also reported that Muslim couples tend to prioritise support from family over professional counselling services. This tendency is largely influenced by cultural values that stress collectivism and the signifi-cance of communal support. For instance, a study conducted among Cana-dian Muslims revealed that although 65% reported experiencing moderate to high psychological distress, only 48.7% had accessed professional treatment. Many chose instead to manage their concerns independently or through sup-port from family and friends (Zia et al., 2022). In a similar theme, research by Tanhan and Young (2022) highlights that Muslims often rely heavily on tra-ditional support mechanisms, including religious and spiritual practices, such as Qur'ân recitation, seeking counsel from a sheikh or *Imam*, prayer, as well as social support networks and lifestyle factors like diet (Tanhan & Young, 2022). These findings highlight the importance of recognising and integrating the role of family and community support in the help-seeking behaviours of Muslim individuals. In Islam, *Fard Kifayah* refers to a communal obligation, an act that, if fulfilled by a sufficient number of people, absolves the rest of the community from responsibility. However, if no one fulfills it, the entire com-munity shares in the accountability and potential sin. This concept extends beyond purely religious duties to encompass broader societal responsibilities, including areas such as education, governance, and healthcare.

Islām places significant emphasis on communal responsibility for individ-ual well-being. Nu'man bin Bashir (may Allāh be pleased with him) reported that the Messenger of Allāh (ﷺ) said, "The believers, in their mutual kindness, compassion, and sympathy, are like one body. When one part of the body suffers, the entire body responds with sleeplessness and fever" (Bukhārī and Muslim). This hadīth powerfully illustrates the Islāmic concept of collective well-being. Just as the body responds to pain in one limb by reacting as a whole, the Muslim community (*Ummah*) is meant to feel and respond to the suffering of any one of its members. This profound sense of interconnectedness is why Muslims, despite their cultural and ethnic diversity, regard one another as brothers and sisters. When a tragedy such as a genocide occurs, the pain is not confined to the directly affected, it resonates throughout the entire Muslim world. This hadīth highlights the core Islāmic values of empathy, solidarity, and mutual care, reinforcing that healing and support are communal responsibilities, not just individual ones. Within the framework of IINT, this principle is put into practice by involving community members, friends, mentors, or faith-based support groups in a person's therapeutic journey. Their involvement offers emotional validation, a sense of belonging, and the social support needed to foster resilience and facilitate recovery.

Religious communities function as vital support systems, helping to alleviate social isolation and enhance emotional well-being. Research consistently shows that participation in congregational activities strengthens social support networks. For instance, McClure (2017) found that engaging in community service through religious organisations promotes prosocial behaviours such as charitable giving and civic involvement. Similarly, Merino (2019) observed that deeper involvement in religious communities enhances social connections and extends networks across diverse groups. In times of hardship, religious communities also offer essential emotional and spiritual support, serving as a protective factor against psychological distress and emotional disorders (Hill & Pargament, 2003). Among African Americans, active participation in faith-based communities has been linked to increased religious social support, including both beneficial and potentially challenging aspects, even within relatively short longitudinal periods (Le et al., 2016). This emphasises the church's role as a powerful social network with meaningful influence on individual lives. Religious social support, often referred to as church-based support, encompasses the assistance individuals receive through their engagement in religious settings. This includes support from clergy as well as fellow congregants, providing access to a unique and spiritually grounded social network (Kanu et al., 2008). Notably, the support offered within religious contexts may differ in both quality and function from that provided by secular networks (Debnam et al., 2012; Krause, 2002). Collectively, these findings highlight the important role that congregational participation plays in fostering meaningful social support, both within religious communities and in broader society.

However, the majority of these studies have focused on non-Muslim populations. Nevertheless, it is reasonable to infer that similar patterns of social support and mental health may be applicable within Muslim communities. Being part of the Muslim community plays a crucial role in mental well-being, as shared religious and cultural values foster a strong sense of identity and belonging. Recent research on Muslim populations has begun to highlight the significant impact of social support on mental health. For instance, Dural et al. (2022) found that among elderly Muslims, higher levels of perceived social support were associated with improved self-care and reduced feelings of loneliness, highlighting its role in promoting overall well-being. Similarly, a study conducted in Iran by Djordjevic et al. (2024) revealed that greater perceived social support correlated with better psychosocial functioning and lower symptom severity in individuals with recent-onset psychosis. Additionally, cultural practices such as *koteba*, a traditional form of theatre in Mali, have been shown to provide therapeutic value by fostering communal support and aiding in the recovery of psychiatric patients (Diallo & Ahmed, 2024). These findings collectively emphasise the critical role of social networks in alleviating loneliness and enhancing mental health among Muslims. The integration of family and community support in the IINT model reflects foundational Islāmic principles of collective healing and social responsibility. By embedding therapeutic practices within familial, communal, and spiritual frameworks, IINT offers a comprehensive and holistic approach to healing. This method not only strengthens social ties and builds emotional resilience but also promotes both individual and collective well-being.

Unlike many Western psychotherapeutic models, which often prioritise individual therapy, IINT recognises that healing occurs within a shared, relational context. Family, friends, and the broader community are seen as essential to an individual's mental and emotional health. Islāmic teachings emphasise the value of social support, mutual consultation (*shūrā*), and shared responsibility in facing life's challenges. As such, IINT ensures that therapy is not an isolated process, but a socially and spiritually integrated journey towards recovery and growth.

The following chapters will explore practical applications such as spiritual interventions, Islāmic storytelling, metaphor use, and clinical strategies tailored to the IINT framework.

References

Abū Dāwūd. *Sunan Abi Dawud 1692*. In-book reference: Book 9, Hadith 137M English translation: Book 9, Hadith 1688. Hasan (Al-Albani) https://sunnah.com/abudawud:1692.

Al-Adab Al-Mufrad 49. *In-book reference : Book 2, Hadith 3*. English translation: Book 2, Hadith 49. Sahih (Al-Albani). https://sunnah.com/adab:49.

Al-Adab Al-Mufrad 54. In-book reference: Book 2, Hadith 8 English translation: Book 2, Hadith 54. Sahih (Al-Albani). https://sunnah.com/adab:54.

Al-Attas, S. M. N. (1995). *Prolegomena to the metaphysics of Islam*. International Institute of Islāmic Thought and Civilization.

A'la Maududi. *Tafseer Tafheem-ul-Quran* Syed Abu-al-A'la Maududi. https://surahquran.com/tafsir-english.php?sora=2&aya=177.

Bukhârî. *Sahih al – Bukhârî 6138*. In-book reference: Book 78, Hadith 165. USC-MSA web (English) reference: Vol. 8, Book 73, Hadith 160.

Carolan, M. T., Basherinia, G., Juhari, R., Himelright, J., & Mouton-Sanders, M. (2000). Contemporary Muslim families: Research and practice. *Contemporary Family Therapy, 22*(1), 67–79.

Debnam, K., Holt, C. L., Clark, E. M., Roth, D. L., & Southward, P. (2012). Relationship between religious social support and general social support with health behaviors in a national sample of African Americans. *Journal of Behavioral Medicine, 35*(2), 179–189. https://doi.org/10.1007/s10865-011-9338-4.

Diallo, M., & Ahmed, B. (2024). *Mali's traditional theater gives psychiatric patients the stage.* https://apnews.com/article/mali-mental-health-theater-psychiatric-art-0c3af0e203263023027f08105799a340

Djordjevic, M., Farhang, S., Shirzadi, M., Mousavi, S. B., Bruggeman, R., Malek, A., Mohagheghi, A., Ranjbar, F., Shafiee-Kandjani, A. R., Jongsma, H. E., & Veling, W. (2024). Self-stigma, religiosity, and perceived social support in people with recent-onset psychosis in the Islāmic Republic of Iran: Associations with symptom severity and psychosocial functioning. *The International Journal of Social Psychiatry, 70*(3), 542–553. https://doi.org/10.1177/00207640231221090.

Dural, G., Kavak Budak, F., Özdemir, A. A., & Gültekin, A. (2022). Effect of perceived social support on self-care *agency and loneliness among elderly Muslim people. Journal of Religion and Health, 61*(2), 1505–1513. https://doi.org/10.1007/s10943-021-01377-5.

Graham, J. R., Bradshaw, C., & Trew, J. L. (2009). Cultural barriers with Muslim clients: An agency perspective. *Administration in Social Work, 33*, 387–406. https://doi.org/10.1080/03643100903172950.

Hill, P. C., & Pargament, K. I. (2003). Advances in the conceptualization and measurement of religion and spirituality. Implications for physical and mental health research. *The American Psychologist, 58*(1), 64–74. https://doi.org/10.1037/0003-066x.58.1.64.

Ibn Kathir. *Quran 2:155 Tafsir Ibn Kathir.* Cited in https://surahquran.com/tafsir-english-aya-155-sora-2.html

Kanu, M., Baker, E., & Brownson, R. C. (2008). Exploring associations between church-based social support and physical activity. *Journal of Physical Activity & Health, 5*(4), 504–515. https://doi.org/10.1123/jpah.5.4.504.

Khan, Z. (2014). *An exploratory study of therapists' practices with Muslim Clients: Building rapport and discussing religion in therapy.* A dissertation submitted to the faculty of the graduate school of applied and professional psychology. Rutgers State University. Submitted in partial fulfilment of the Requirements for the degree of Doctor of Psychology. https://www.academia.edu/125014008/An_exploratory_study_of_therapists_practices_with_muslim_clients_Building_rapport_and_discussing_religion_in_therapy

Krause, N. (2002). Church-based social support and health in old age: Exploring variations by race. *The Journals of Gerontology. Series B, Psychological Sciences and Social Sciences, 57*(6), S332–S347. https://doi.org/10.1093/geronb/57.6.s332.

Le, D., Holt, C. L., Hosack, D. P., Huang, J., & Clark, E. M. (2016). Religious participation is associated with increases in religious social support in a national longitudinal study of African Americans. *Journal of Religion and Health, 55*(4), 1449–1460. https://doi.org/10.1007/s10943-015-0143-1.

Merino, S. M. (2019). Religious involvement and bridging social ties: The role of congregational participation. *Socio-Historical Examination of Religion and Ministry, 1*(2), 291–308. https://doi.org/10.33929/sherm.2019.vol1.no2.10.

McClure, J. M. (2017). "Go and Do Likewise": Investigating whether involvement in congregationally sponsored community service activities predicts prosocial behavior. *Review of Religious Research, 59*(3), 341–366. https://doi.org/10.1007/s13644-017-0290-9 (Original work published 2017).

Phillips, A. A. B. (1994). *The fundamentals of Tawheed (Islāmic Monotheism)*. International Islāmic Publishing House.

Rassool, G. Hussein. (2019). *Evil eye, Jinn possession and mental health issues: An Islāmic perspective*. Routledge.

Rassool, G. Hussein. (2021). *Islāmic psychology: Human behaviour and experiences from an Islāmic perspective*. Routledge.

Rassool, G. Hussein. (2024a). *Exploring the intersection of Islāmic spiritual and psychotherapy: Healing the soul*. Springer.

Rassool, G. Hussein. (2024b). *Monotheism as the foundation of Islāmic psychotherapy*. In *Exploring the intersection of Islāmic spirituality and psychotherapy*. Springer 15–26. https://doi.org/10.1007/978-3-031-72724-5_2

Rassool, G. Hussein. (2024c). *Spiritual integration in Islāmic psychotherapy: Unveiling the therapist's soul*. Focus Series. Islāmic Psychology and Psychotherapy. Routledge.

Springer, P. R., Abbott, D. A., & Reisbig, A. M. J. (2009). Therapy with Muslim couples and families: Basic guidelines for effective practice. *The Family Journal: Counseling and Therapy for Couples and Family, 17*, 229–235. https://doi.org/10.1177/1066480709337798.

Tanhan, A., & Young, J. S. (2022). Muslims and mental health services: A concept map and a theoretical framework. *Journal of Religion and Health, 61*(1), 23–63. https://doi.org/10.1007/s10943-021-01324-4

Zia, B., Abdulrazaq, S., & Mackenzie, C. S. (2022). Mental health service utilization and psychological help-seeking preferences among Canadian Muslims. *Canadian Journal of Community Mental Health, 41*(1), 35–45. https://doi.org/10.7870/cjcmh-2022-003.

5 Spiritual interventions in Islāmic Integrated Narrative Therapy model

Introduction

Islāmic Integrated Narrative Therapy (IINT) is an approach that harmonises the principles of narrative therapy with Islāmic teachings, offering a model that is both culturally and spiritually aligned with the needs of Muslim clients. Within the framework of Islāmic psychology, spiritual interventions are central to the processes of healing, transformation, and meaning-making. Healing in IINT is viewed holistically, and spiritual healing is at the heart of its methodology. Core Islāmic spiritual practices such as *dhikr* (remembrance of Allāh), *du'āh* (supplication), *salāh* (prayer), *sadaqah* (charity), and *ruqyah* (incantation) are integral to this healing process. These interventions aim to restore harmony between the mind, body, and spirit, fostering emotional resilience and psychological well-being. Spiritual interventions in IINT are not supplementary, but foundational. They offer clients a pathway to reconnect with their faith, draw strength from spiritual narratives, and reinterpret their struggles through an Islāmic worldview. By integrating these elements, IINT transcends the boundaries of conventional therapy, recognising the essential role of spirituality in shaping human experiences, coping strategies, and overall mental health. This chapter will explore the therapeutic role of key spiritual intervention, including *dhikr*, *du'āh*, *salāh*, *sadaqah*, and *ruqya*, highlighting how each contributes to the transformative journey within the IINT framework.

Dhikr (remembrance of Allāh)

Dhikr, or the remembrance of Allāh, involves the recitation of His names and attributes as a means of praise and spiritual reflection. Rooted deeply in Islāmic spirituality, this practice serves as a powerful tool for calming the heart, reducing stress, and strengthening one's connection with the Creator. *Dhikr* takes many forms, including the recitation of the Qur'ân and the repetition of specific phrases that seek divine forgiveness and glorify Allāh. Common expressions include *Astaghfirullāh* (I seek forgiveness from Allāh),

DOI: 10.4324/9781003584995-6

Subḥān Allāh (Glory be to Allāh), *Alḥamdulillāh* (Praise be to Allāh), *Lā ilāha illa Allāh* (There is no deity but Allāh), *Allāhu Akbar* (Allāh is the Greatest), and *Lā ḥawla wa lā quwwata illā billāh* (There is no power nor strength except with Allāh). Additionally, the invocation of Allāh's beautiful names further deepens the spiritual impact of *dhikr*. Dhikr is believed to have a therapeutic effect on the mind, helping individuals overcome feelings of anxiety, sadness, or inner turmoil. Allāh says in the Qur'ân:

$$\text{أَلَا بِذِكْرِ ٱللَّهِ تَطْمَئِنُّ ٱلْقُلُوبُ}$$

- *Unquestionably, by the remembrance of Allah do hearts are assured.*
  (Ar-Ra'd 13:28, interpretation of the meaning)

According to the exegesis of Ibn Kathīr (2000), "(Those who believed, and whose hearts find rest in the remembrance of Allah.) for their hearts find comfort on the side of Allah, become tranquil when He is remembered and pleased to have Him as their Protector and Supporter." This verse underscores the calming and reassuring effect of *dhikr*, highlighting its potential as a powerful spiritual intervention in therapeutic settings.

Empirical studies further support the psychological and physiological benefits of *dhikr*. For instance, an Egyptian study by Solman and Mohamed (2013) investigated the effects of repeating short religious phrases in combination with jaw relaxation techniques on post-operative pain. The findings indicated a reduction in anxiety among the intervention group, although the impact on pain relief was inconclusive. However, the study has been critique, most notably by Mayberry (2020, for lacking a comparable non-religious educational programme for the control group, which limits the strength of its conclusions. Other research also affirms the efficacy of *dhikr* in various therapeutic contexts. Natori (2017) found that *Asmaul Husna dhikr* therapy enhanced self-control in individuals with alcohol dependence. Similarly, *dhikr* has been shown to reduce pain (Mualamat et al., 2020), alleviate stress (Nosrati et al., 2021), and improve sleep quality when incorporated into a *dhikr*-based breathing relaxation model (Purwanto et al., 2022). Moreover, Irhas et al. (2023) noted that *dhikr* can have a profound effect on an individual's intellectual, emotional, and spiritual well-being. In the context of chronic illness, Syahri et al. (2024) demonstrated that *dhikr* therapy significantly improves the quality of life for cancer patients, particularly in the physical, emotional, and spiritual dimensions.

Du ʿāh (supplication)

Du ʿāh refers to supplication or the act of calling upon Allāh for help, guidance, and healing. It is a direct and intimate way of asking for divine intervention. Ibn al-Qayyim Al-Jawziyyah states that *du ʿāh* is one of the most effective remedies. It acts as a powerful shield against adversity, capable of warding off calamities, healing them, preventing their occurrence, or lessening their impact if they do occur. It is considered the believer's ultimate weapon (Cited in Wyatt, 2020). In IINT, *du'āh* serves as a means for clients to express their fears, hopes, desires, and gratitude to Allāh, allowing them to experience emotional release and spiritual comfort.

وَإِذَا سَأَلَكَ عِبَادِى عَنِّى فَإِنِّى قَرِيبٌ ۖ أُجِيبُ دَعْوَةَ ٱلدَّاعِ إِذَا دَعَانِ ۖ فَلْيَسْتَجِيبُواْ لِى وَلْيُؤْمِنُواْ بِى لَعَلَّهُمْ يَرْشُدُونَ

- *And when My servants ask you [O Muhammad], concerning Me, indeed I am near. I respond to the invocation of the supplicant when he calls upon Me... So let them respond to Me [by obedience] and believe in Me, perhaps they will be [rightly] guided.* (Al-Baqarah 2:186, interpretation of the meaning)

Referring to the above verse, Ala' Maududi in his exegesis stated that

Although you cannot see Me nor perceive Me with your senses, yet you must never imagine that I am far from you. Nay, I am so near to every servant of Mine that he can invoke Me and place his request before Me wherever he is. So much so that I hear and answer even those requests which are not expressed in words but are made only in the innermost heart. As to the false and impotent gods you have created in your ignorance and folly, you have to travel co them, and even then they do not hear and answer you. But here am I, the Sovereign, the absolute Ruler of the boundless universe and Possessor of all powers and authority, so near to hear and answer you that you need no recommendation of intercession for making any request anywhere at any time you like. Therefore you should free yourselves from the folly of running from door to door after false gods, and accept My invitation and turn to Me and trust in Me and submit to Me and become My servants.

This verse assures that Allāh listens to the supplications of His servants, offering hope and healing through sincere *du'āh*. It was narrated from an-Nu'maan ibn Basheer (may Allah be pleased with him) that the Messenger of Allah 🌺 said: "Du'āh is worship." Then he recited the verse (interpretation of the meaning): "And your Lord says, 'Call upon Me; I will respond to you.' Indeed, those who disdain My worship will enter Hell [rendered] contemptible" [Ghaafir 40:60] (Ahmad & Bukhârî).

Allah says in the Qur'ân:

ٱدْعُونِىٓ أَسْتَجِبْ لَكُمْ ۚ

- *And your Lord says, 'Call upon Me; I will respond to you'.''* (Ghafir 40:60)

This verse carries profound psychological and spiritual significance. Spiritually, it affirms Allah's mercy and accessibility, encouraging believers to seek solace through *du 'āh* while maintaining a balance between effort and reliance. From a psychological perspective, it fosters emotional expression, offering a therapeutic outlet similar to self-disclosure, which alleviates distress and strengthens resilience. It instils a sense of security, hope, and agency, countering feelings of helplessness by reinforcing trust in divine wisdom (*tawakkul*).

Research on the effectiveness of prayer has revealed a wide range of psychological, physiological, neuroscientific, and social benefits. Evidence suggests that individuals who pray to a compassionate and protective deity are less prone to anxiety-related disorders such as chronic worry, fear, self-consciousness, social anxiety, and obsessive-compulsive behaviours, compared to those who engage in prayer without expecting comfort or divine support (Ellison et al., 2014). In a study referenced by Sadaf (2024), Newberg found notable differences in brain activity between religious individuals before and after prayer, and atheists before and after meditation. Regular prayer has been linked to reduced symptoms of depression and anxiety (Koenig, 2012), greater optimism, and lower stress levels (Ai et al., 2002). It also appears to enhance self-control and patience (Friese & Wänke, 2014). Physiological studies further support these findings, showing that prayer can help lower blood pressure and improve cardiovascular health (Benson et al., 2006), lessen pain perception, and accelerate recovery (Wachholtz & Pargament, 2005). Additionally, prayer has been found to strengthen the immune system by reducing inflammatory markers such as interleukin-6 (Lutgendorf et al., 2004).

From a neuroscientific perspective, prayer activates areas of the brain involved in emotional regulation, contributing to improved emotional stability (Newberg et al., 2003). It also triggers the release of dopamine, a neurotransmitter associated with reward and well-being (Schjødt et al., 2008). Socially, prayer has been associated with enhanced social bonds, decreased feelings of loneliness (Ellison & Levin, 1998), healthier lifestyle habits, and a reduction in substance abuse (Wallace & Forman, 1998). Together, these studies present compelling evidence that prayer can significantly benefit mental, physical, and social health.

Despite these promising findings, some research highlights potential negative outcomes and underscores the need for further investigation. Notably, much of the current literature centres on Judeo-Christian populations, with limited research exploring the impact of prayer in Muslim communities. Fenwick (2004) emphasised the need for future research to focus on formalising and quantifying prayer practices, suggesting that standardising the mental intent behind prayer could yield more consistent and reliable outcomes.

Ṣalāh (prayer)

Ṣalāh or the Islāmic prayer is not merely a physical act of worship but also a profound psychological and spiritual practice. As one of the Five Pillars of

Islam, it is an essential act of devotion that plays a central role in the life of a Muslim. Allah says in the Qur'ân:

وَٱسْتَعِينُوٓاْ بِٱلصَّبْرِ وَٱلصَّلَوٰةِ ۚ وَإِنَّهَا لَكَبِيرَةٌ إِلَّا عَلَى ٱلْخَٰشِعِينَ

- *And seek help through patience and prayer. And indeed, it is a difficult except for the humbly submissive[to Allah].* (Al-Baqarah 2:45, interpretation of the meaning):

In the Tafsir of Al-Jalalayn (a), the above verse is explained as follows:

Seek help ask for assistance in your affairs in patience by restraining the soul in the face of that which it dislikes; and prayer. The singling out of this for mention is a way of emphasising its great importance; in one *hadīth* it is stated "When something bothered the Prophet (ﷺ) he would immediately resort to prayer."

This verse emphasises that prayer (*ṣalāh*) is a source of strength and spiritual resilience, offering a means to seek help from Allāh in times of difficulty. Performed five times a day as a mandatory act, *salāh* is structured into specific intervals, providing regular opportunities for reflection and contemplation. Each prayer begins with the intention (*niyyah*), setting the stage for a contemplative, focused experience.

فَإِذَا قَضَيْتُمُ ٱلصَّلَوٰةَ فَٱذْكُرُواْ ٱللَّهَ قِيَٰمًا وَقُعُودًا وَعَلَىٰ جُنُوبِكُمْ ۚ فَإِذَا ٱطْمَأْنَنتُمْ فَأَقِيمُواْ ٱلصَّلَوٰةَ ۚ إِنَّ ٱلصَّلَوٰةَ كَانَتْ عَلَى ٱلْمُؤْمِنِينَ كِتَٰبًا مَّوْقُوتًا

- *And when you have completed the prayers are over, remember Allāh standing, sitting, or [lying] on your sides. But when you become secure, re-establish [regular] prayers. Indeed, prayers has been decreed upon the believers a decree of specified times.* (An-Nisa, 4:103, interpretation of the meaning)

In his exegesis of the above verse, Muhammad Taqiud-Din Al Hilali explained that

When you have finished *As-Ṣalāh* (the prayer – congregational), remember Allāh standing, sitting down, and lying down on your sides, but when you are free from danger, perform *As-Ṣalāh* (*Iqamat-as-salāh*). Verily, the prayer is enjoined on the believers at fixed hours.

The physical movements in *salāh*, such as bowing (*ruku*) and prostration (*sujood*), combined with the recitation of Qur'ānic verses, offer a dual benefit, promoting both physical ease and mental calm. Prostration, which symbolises complete submission and humility before Allāh, the Almighty, has been found to produce a grounding, soothing effect that helps reduce stress. The rhythmic sequence of movements and recitations encourages a meditative state, enhancing mental clarity and relieving anxiety, similar to the benefits observed in other contemplative practices. Furthermore, *salāh* fosters a strong sense of community, particularly when performed in congregation. This shared act of worship provides emotional support, strengthens social bonds, and helps diminish feelings of loneliness. In essence, *salāh* is not only a profound spiritual connection with the Divine but also a powerful psychospiritual practice that supports stress relief, emotional balance, and mental well-being.

Beyond its spiritual significance, *salāh* has garnered increasing attention for its potential impact on mental, physical, and emotional well-being. In terms of mental health outcomes, Ijaz et al. (2017) found a significant association between regular practice of *salāh* and enhanced psychological well-being, with individuals who pray regularly demonstrating better mental health compared to non-practitioners. Likewise, Owens et al. (2023) emphasised the role of *salāh*, along with supplicatory prayer, Qur'ānic recitation, reading, memorisation, and listening, in reducing symptoms of anxiety, depression, and stress, while simultaneously improving quality of life and coping mechanisms. A broader body of research has highlighted the strong link between prayer and overall health. Mayberry (2020) noted a stark contrast between the focus of prayer-related studies conducted in the West and those in Iran. In Western contexts, there has been a tendency to evaluate the clinical effectiveness of prayer, seeking to establish its therapeutic potential as comparable to medication and, by extension, as evidence of a higher power or transcendent force affecting health outcomes. In contrast, Iranian studies have concentrated more on the psychological benefits of prayer, advocating for greater openness among clinicians to its supportive role and even encouraging them to pray for their patients (Mayberry, 2020, p. 5). This distinction reflects differing cultural and philosophical approaches to incorporating spirituality into healthcare. In Pakistan, patient attitudes further highlight the integration of spirituality and medical care. In one study, 93% of patients expressed a desire for their doctors to pray for them, and 88% believed that having a God-fearing physician would positively influence their health (Ahmed et al., 2007). Another study reported that 96% of patients believed in the healing power of prayer, with 90% claiming to have personally experienced healing through it (Qidwai et al., 2009). Additionally, evidence shows that many patients use prayer alongside conventional medical treatment (Ateeq et al., 2014), reflecting its complementary role in healthcare.

Numerous studies have explored the relationship between prayer and health outcomes. Byrd's landmark study (2000) on distant intercessory prayer in coronary care units found that patients who were prayed for required fewer medical interventions, such as ventilatory support and antibiotics, though there was no significant difference in mortality rates. Iranian research has also indicated positive effects of prayer, including prayers attributed to the

Prophet, in improving health outcomes (Nasiri, 2010). A study by Alwasiti et al. (2010) examining the effects of a 5–9 minute prayer session revealed increased alpha brainwave activity during the *sujood* (prostration) phase. Alpha waves are typically linked to relaxed and focused mental states, similar to those induced by meditation or concentrated contemplation (Newberg et al., 2015), suggesting that the act of prostration may foster a calm and mentally centred state.

Prayer is also commonly utilised in countries like Iran and Turkey, particularly among cancer patients, where spiritual healing has been reported to enhance well-being and relieve symptoms (Golestan, 2014; Rahnama et al., 2012). In another study, individuals who engaged in prayer during midlife were found to have a lower risk of developing mild cognitive impairment, though no similar benefit was observed for the prevention of Alzheimer's disease (Sabbagh et al., 2012). Other research, including studies on patients in comas or those with carpal tunnel syndrome, has produced mixed results, often due to small sample sizes and methodological weaknesses (Nasiri, 2010; Sabbagh et al., 2012). In the context of the American population, Upenieks (2023) found that devotional prayers, especially those focused on praising God or praying for the well-being of others, along with prayer expectancies (beliefs about whether prayers are answered), were associated with lower levels of anxiety.

Collectively, these studies point towards the potential of prayer to enhance mental health, reduce anxiety, and promote general well-being. However, limitations such as insufficient control groups and variability in personal prayer practices (Nasiri, 2010) should be carefully considered when interpreting the findings.

Sadaqah (charity)

Sadaqah, or voluntary charity, is a spiritual practice in Islām that not only benefits the receiver but also purifies the heart of the giver. Allāh says in the Qur'ân:

مَّثَلُ ٱلَّذِينَ يُنفِقُونَ أَمْوَٰلَهُمْ فِى سَبِيلِ ٱللَّهِ كَمَثَلِ حَبَّةٍ أَنۢبَتَتْ سَبْعَ سَنَابِلَ فِى كُلِّ سُنۢبُلَةٍ مِّا۟ئَةُ حَبَّةٍ ۗ وَٱللَّهُ يُضَٰعِفُ لِمَن يَشَآءُ ۚ وَٱللَّهُ وَٰسِعٌ عَلِيمٌ

- *The example of those who spend their wealth in the way of Allah is like a seed [of grain] which grows seven spikes; in each spike is a hundred grains. And Allah multiplies [His reward] for whom He wills. And Allah is all-Encompassing and Knowing.* (Al-Baqarah 2:261, interpretation of the meaning)

According to Tafsīr al-Jalālayn (b), this verse reflects that charity given sincerely in Allah's path is multiplied immensely, up to 700 times, signifying both divine reward and spiritual cleansing. Charity serves not only as worship but also as a therapeutic act. It fosters emotional resilience, reduces stress, and promotes psychological well-being. The Qur'ān further affirms: Allah says in the Qur'ân:

خُذْ مِنْ أَمْوَٰلِهِمْ صَدَقَةً تُطَهِّرُ هُمْ وَتُزَكِّيهِم بِهَا وَصَلِّ عَلَيْهِمْ ۖ إِنَّ صَلَوٰتَكَ سَكَنٌ لَّهُمْ

- *Take, [O, Muhammad], from their wealth a charity by which you purify them and cause them increase, and invoke [Allah's blessings] upon them.* (At-Tawbah 9:103, interpretation of the meaning)

Almuntakhab Fi Tafsir Alqur'an Alkarim interprets this as charity, setting one upon the path of purity and mental peace, helping free the mind from guilt and spiritual disturbance. Al-Jurjānī emphasied the recommendation of giving charity after committing a sin, in line with:

إِنَّ ٱلْحَسَنَٰتِ يُذْهِبْنَ ٱلسَّيِّئَاتِ ۚ ذَٰلِكَ

- *Indeed, good deeds do away with misdeeds.* (Hid 11:114, interpretation of the meaning)

This verse highlights the powerful effect of performing good deeds. It suggests that good actions can counterbalance and wipe out the consequences of previous sins or bad deeds. This is reinforced in another verse of the Qur'ân. Allāh says:

إِن تُبْدُوا۟ ٱلصَّدَقَٰتِ فَنِعِمَّا هِيَ ۖ وَإِن تُخْفُوهَا وَتُؤْتُوهَا ٱلْفُقَرَآءَ فَهُوَ خَيْرٌ لَّكُمْ ۚ وَيُكَفِّرُ عَنكُم مِّن سَيِّئَاتِكُمْ ۗ وَٱللَّهُ بِمَا تَعْمَلُونَ خَبِيرٌ

- *If you disclose your charitable expenditures, they are good; but if you conceal them and give them to the poor, it is better for you, and He will remove from you some of your misdeeds [thereby]. And Allah, with what you do, is [fully] Acquainted.* (Al-Baqarah 2:271, interpretation of the meaning)

Ibn Jarīr explains this as charity expiating sins. The Prophet ﷺ echoed this principle when he said: "Have taqwa of Allah wherever you may be, and follow up a bad deed with a good deed which will wipe it out…" (Tirmidhī). It was narrated that Mu'adh bin Jabal said: The Messenger of Allah (ﷺ) stated that "And charity extinguishes sin as water extinguishes fire…" (Ibn Majah(a)).

Psychologically, engaging in charitable acts has been shown to reduce stress and improve overall well-being. Mohseni and Bighash (2020) analytically demonstrated that charity brings both worldly and spiritual benefits, such as prosperity, divine favour, and peace in the Hereafter, which in turn enhance mental wellness and life satisfaction. Scientific studies reinforce these findings. Raposa et al. (2016) observed that acts of giving lower cortisol levels, a key stress hormone, and improve emotional regulation. Harbaugh et al. (2007) found that giving activates brain reward pathways, increasing feelings of happiness and fulfillment. Similarly, Musick and Wilson (2003) and Dulin and Hill (2003) noted that charitable behaviours correlate with reduced depression and more effective coping strategies, especially in religious settings. Post (2005) also found a link between regular charity and increased physical health and longevity.

Islamic charitable practices like *zakāt* (obligatory almsgiving) and waqf (endowment for public welfare) have also shown notable psychological benefits. *Zakāt*, one of the five pillars of Islām, fosters traits like sincerity and compassion. Masroom et al. (2020) highlighted that understanding the spiritual wisdom behind *zakāt* is essential for psychological well-being, as it builds gratitude and emotional balance. The practice of *waqf*, the endowment of assets for ongoing public welfare, too, provides spiritual reward and emotional comfort. Baqutayan et al. (2018) found that those engaging in waqf reported increased happiness, inner peace, and self-satisfaction. More broadly, Nur Afifah et al. (2023) proposed ṣadaqah therapy, emphasising that voluntary charity fosters contentment, reduces stress, and cultivates virtues like gratitude and character development. Among practicing Muslims, there's a strong belief in charity's healing powers. A study by Qidwai et al. (2010) revealed that 85% of patients gave charity hoping for physical healing, while 92% saw it as religiously significant. Participants believed ṣadaqah not only contributed to recovery but shortened illness duration, boosted immunity, and even prolonged life. These findings highlight the integration of *ṣadaqah* into health beliefs, emphasising its value in holistic care. Clinicians aware of this spiritual practice can form stronger therapeutic alliances and improve patient outcomes by respecting these beliefs.

Ruqyah (incantations)

Ruqyah refers to spiritual healing through the recitation of Qur'ānic verses and supplications, often used for spiritual afflictions, *jinn* possession, and chronic ailments. In English, it's often translated as "incantation," though this can misleadingly imply magic, something explicitly prohibited in Islām. The Qur'ān describes itself as a healing source:

وَنُنَزِّلُ مِنَ ٱلْقُرْءَانِ مَا هُوَ شِفَآءٌ وَرَحْمَةٌ لِّلْمُؤْمِنِينَ ۚ

- *And We send down of the Qur'ân hat which is healing and mercy for the believers* (Al Isra' 17.82, interpretation of the meaning)

قُلْ هُوَ لِلَّذِينَ ءَامَنُوا۟ هُدًى وَشِفَآءٌ ۖ

- *"Say: It is for those who believe, guidance and cure."* (Fussilat 41.44, interpretation of the meaning)

In another verse of the Qur'ān, Allāh says:

يَٰٓأَيُّهَا ٱلنَّاسُ قَدْ جَآءَتْكُم مَّوْعِظَةٌ مِّن رَّبِّكُمْ وَشِفَآءٌ لِّمَا فِى ٱلصُّدُورِ وَهُدًى

- *O mankind, there has to come to you instruction from your Lord and healing for what is in the breasts.* (Yunus, 10:57, interpretation of the meaning)

These verses reflect the Qur'ān's ability to soothe emotional and psychological distress, guide spiritual well-being, and address inner turmoil. Authentic narrations affirm the use of Qur'ānic healing. ʿĀishah (may Allāh be pleased with her) reported that the Prophet (ﷺ) would recite the *Muʿawwidhāt* (the last three sūrahs) and blow over himself when ill (Ibn Mājah). Abu Saʿīd al-Khudrī used *Sūrat al-Fātiḥah* to cure a man from a scorpion sting, later confirmed by the Prophet (ﷺ): "How did you know that Sūrat al-Fātiḥah is a *ruqyah*?" (Bukhārī). While *ruqyah* is sometimes mistranslated as "incantations," Islām defines it strictly as healing rooted in *tawḥīd*, avoiding shirk. *Ruqyah* is divided into two forms: *Ruqyah Ash-Sharʿiyyah* (permissible, grounded in Qur'ān and Sunnah) and Ruqyah Ash-*Shirkiyyah* (prohibited). For deeper context, see Rassool (2019) and Latif et al. (2014). Ameen (2005) outlined criteria for spiritual healers: strong *īmān*, Qur'ānic knowledge, sincerity, patient confidentiality, and no pursuit of fame or financial gain. They must also understand mental health to refer cases appropriately to qualified professionals.

Though empirical research is limited, several studies, primarily from Malaysia, show promising results. Saskia et al. (2022) found *ruqyah* offers spiritual protection, reduces anxiety, and supports healing when free from shirk. It strengthens dhikr, instils peace, and can manage emotional imbalance. Shuluddin (2016) reported improvement in conditions like gastritis, migraines, tonsillitis, cancer, and even HIV when *ruqyah* was combined with ḥalāl nutrition and medical care. Mental health outcomes are also promising. Arifuddin and Pamungkas (2018) noted reduced anxiety, stress, and depression in students. Mohamad and Othman (2016) found *ruqyah* beneficial for individuals with depression. A breast cancer study showed reduced proliferation of cancer cells in the treatment group, suggesting physiological benefits. Ja'afar et al., (2021) demonstrated positive behavioural changes in children with autism after ruqyah therapy. Rahman and Hussin (2021) documented a British Pakistani man suffering from cluster headaches. Initially reliant on morphine, he turned to ruqyah therapy and saw dramatic improvements, eventually discontinuing morphine entirely. This case illustrates ruqyah's potential in treating physical conditions and highlights the need for collaboration between healthcare providers and religious practitioners. Al Ghaffayr et al. (2020) support integrating *ruqyah* into modern healthcare as a complementary approach. It enhances well-being, comfort, and cultural congruence for Muslim patients. Future research should investigate its broader therapeutic value and integration into evidence-based mental health models.

Conclusion

IINT places spiritual healing at its core, recognising it as a vital component of psychological and emotional well-being. Key Islamic spiritual practices, such as *dhikr* (remembrance of Allāh), *duʿā'h* (supplication), *salāh* (prayer), *ṣadaqah* (charity), and *ruqyah* (Qur'anic healing, play essential roles in this therapeutic process. By incorporating these practices into the therapeutic framework, IINT not only supports emotional and psychological recovery but also nurtures an individual's faith, resilience, and spiritual connection with Allāh. This holistic approach affirms that genuine healing encompasses the mind, heart, and soul – promoting comprehensive well-being and spiritual fulfillment.

References

Afifah, N., Nindi Ramadhani, K. D., & Salsabila, A. (2023). *Benefits of Sodaqoh [sadaqah] therapy in Islāmic psychotherapy against jealousy.* Vol. 2 (2023): Proceeding Conference on Da'wah and Communication Studies. https://doi.org/10.61994/cdcs. v2i1.101.

Ahmad in al-Musnad (18352) and al- Bukhârî in *al-Adab al-Mufrad (714).* Cited in Islamqa (2020). Du`a is worship. https://islamqa.info/en/answers/320772/dua-is-worship

Ahmed, W., Choudhry, A. M., Alam. A. Y., & Kaisar, F. (2007). Muslim patients' perceptions of faith-based healing and religious inclination of treating physicians. *Pakistan Heart Journal, 40*(3), 61–65.

Ai, A. L., Peterson, C., Bolling, S. F., & Koenig, H. (2002). Private prayer and optimism in middle-aged and older patients awaiting cardiac surgery. *The Gerontologist, 42*(1), 70–81.

Al Ghaffayr, M. I. S., Habibi, A. Z., Ridho, S., Sari, D. et al. (2020). *Re-reading Ruqyah: Comprehensive analysis of Ruqyah within Hadith, medicine, and psychological perspective.* Proceedings of the 3rd International Colloquium on Interdisciplinary Islāmic Studies, ICIIS 2020, 20–21 October 2020, Jakarta, Indonesia. https://eudl. eu/doi/10.4108/eai.20-10-2020.2305139.

Al-Jalalayn (a). *Qur'ân 2:45 Tafsir Al-Jalalayn.* https://surahquran.com/tafsir-english-aya-45-sora-2.html

Al-Jalalayn (b). *Qur'ân 2:261 Tafsir Al-Jalalayn.* https://surahquran.com/tafsir-english. php?sora=2&aya=261

Al-Jarjaani in Mughni al-Muhtaaj (3/206). Cited in Islam Q&A (2011). *Is it prescribed for the one who commits a sin to give charity after that?* https://islamqa.info/en/ answers/146238/ruling-on-giving-charity-after-every-sin

Almuntakhab Fi Tafsir Alquran Alkarim. Qur'ân 9:103. https://surahquran.com/ tafsir-english.php?sora=9&aya=103

Alwasiti, H., Aris, I. B., & Jantan, A. B. (2010). EEG activity in Muslim prayer: A pilot study. *Maejo International Journal of Science and Technology, 4*, 496–511.

Ameen, Abu'l-Mundhir Khaleel ibn Ibraaheem. (2005). *The jinn and human sickness: Remedies in the light of the Qur'ân and Sunnah.* Darussalam Publications.

Arifuddin, W. Y., & Pamungkas, A. Y. F. (2018). The effect of Ruqyah Syar'iyyah therapy on anxiety, stress and depression among health science students. *Journal of Holistic Nursing and Health Science, 1*(2). https://ejournal2.undip.ac.id/index.php/ hnhs

Ateeq, M., Jehan, S., & Mehmood, R. J. (2014). Faith healing, modern health care. *Professional Medical Journal, 21*(2), 295–230.

64   *Islāmic Integrated Narrative Therapy*

Baqutayan, S. M. S., Mohsin, M. I. A., Mahdzir, A. M., & Ariffin, A. S. (2018). The psychology of giving behavior in Islam. *Sociology International Journal, 2*(2),88–92. https://doi.org/10.15406/sij.2018.02.00037.

Benson, H., Dusek, J. A., Sherwood, J. B., Lam, P., Bethea, C. F., Carpenter, W., Levitsky, S., Hill, P. C., Clem, D. W., Jr, Jain, M. K., Drumel, D., Kopecky, S. L., Mueller, P. S., Marek, D., Rollins, S., & Hibberd, P. L. (2006). Study of the Therapeutic Effects of Intercessory Prayer (STEP) in cardiac bypass patients: A multicenter randomized trial of uncertainty and certainty of receiving intercessory prayer. *American Heart Journal, 151*(4), 934–942. https://doi.org/10.1016/j.ahj.2005.05.028.

Byrd, R. C. (2000). The power of prayer: Randomized, controlled trial of intercessory prayer in the coronary care unit. *Southern Medical Journal, 93*(9), 941–944.

Dulin, P. L., & Hill, R. D. (2003). Relationships between altruistic activity and positive and negative affect among low-income older adult service providers. *Aging & Mental Health, 7*(4), 294–299. https://doi.org/10.1080/1360786031000120697.

Ellison, C. G., Bradshaw, M., Flannelly, K. J., & Galek, K. C. (2014). Prayer, attachment to god, and symptoms of anxiety-related disorders among U.S. Adults. *Sociology of Religion, 75*(2), 208–233. https://www.jstor.org/stable/24580197.

Ellison, C. G., & Levin, J. S. (1998). The religion-health connection: Evidence, theory, and future directions. *Health Education & Behavior: The Official Publication of the Society for Public Health Education, 25*(6), 700–720. https://doi.org/10.1177/109019819802500603.

Fenwick, P. (2004). *Scientific evidence for the efficacy of prayer*. Roal College of Psychiatrist. www.rcpsych.ac.uk/docs/default-source/members/sigs/spirituality-spsig/resource.

Friese, M., & Wänke, M. (2014). Personal prayer buffers self-control depletion. *Journal of Experimental Social Psychology, 51,* 56–59. https://doi.org/10.1016/j.jesp.2013.11.006.

Golestan, S. (2014). Effects of spiritual practices on well-being in cancer patients. *Journal of Islāmic and Complementary Medicine, 3*(2), 212–220.

Harbaugh, W. T., Mayr, U., & Burghart, D. R. (2007). Neural responses to taxation and voluntary giving reveal motives for charitable donations. *Science (New York, N.Y.), 316*(5831), 1622–1625. https://doi.org/10.1126/science.1140738.

Ibn Kathir. (2000). *Tafsir ibn Kathir* (Trans. J. Abualrub, N. Khitab, H. Khitab, A. Walker, M. Al-Jibali, & S. Ayoub). Darussalam Publishers and Distributors.

Ibn Majah (a). *Sunan Ibn Majah 3973.* In-book reference: Book 36, Hadith 48. English translation: Vol. 5, Book 36, Hadith 3973. Hasan (Darussalam. https://sunnah.com/ibnmajah:3973/.

Ibn Majah (b). *Sunan Ibn Majah 3529.* In-book reference: Book 31, Hadith 94. English translation: Vol. 4, Book 31, Hadith 3529. Sahih (Darussalam). https://sunnah.com/ibnmajah:3529.

Ijaz, S., Khalily, M. T., & Ahmad, I. (2017). Mindfulness in Salah prayer and its association with mental health. *Journal of Religion and Health, 56,* 2297–2307.

Irhas, I., Aziz, A. A., & Satriawan, L. A. (2023). The power of Dhikr: Elevating intellectual, emotional, and spiritual quotients. *Al-Hayat: Journal of Islāmic Education, [S.l.], 7*(2), 601–610.

Ja'afar, N., Rezki Perdani Sawai, & Joki Perdani Sawai. (2021). Ruqyah Syariyyah and the emotional regulation of children with autism. *Journal of Quran Sunnah Education & Special Needs, 5*(2), 18–27. https://doi.org/10.33102/jqss.vol5no2.115.

Koenig, H. G. (2012). *Religion, spirituality, and health: The research and clinical implications.* ISRN Psychiatry, 2012, 278730.

Latif, J., Dockrat, S., & Rassool, G. Hussein. (2024). *Integrating spiritual interventions in islāmic psychology: A practical guide.* Focus Series on Islāmic Psychology & Psychotherapy. Routledge.

Lutgendorf, S. K., Russell, D., Ullrich, P., Harris, T. B., & Wallace, R. (2004). Religious participation, interleukin-6, and mortality in older adults. *Health Psychology: Official Journal of the Division of Health Psychology, American Psychological Association, 23*(5), 465–475. https://doi.org/10.1037/0278-6133.23.5.465.

Masroom, M. N., Wan Mohd Azam Wan Mohd Yunus, & Miftachul, Huda. (2020). Understanding of significance of Zakat (Islāmic Charity) for psychological well-being. *Journal of Critical Reviews, 7*(2), 693–697.

Mayberry, J. F. (2020). Health, prayer and spirituality: A review of the Muslim contribution. *BIMA: Journal of the British Islāmic Medical Association, 5*(2), 1–8.

Mohamad, M. A., & Othman, N. (2016). The Ruqyah Syar'iyyah spiritual method as an alternative for depression treatment. *Mediterranean Journal of Social Sciences, 7*(4), 406, 411.

Mohseni, T., & Bighash, K. A. (2020). Psychological effects of charitable activities on the worldly mental health and eternal happiness of the hereafter from the perspective of the Qur'an and Hadith. *International Journal of Multicultural and Multireligious Understanding, 7*(6), 180–196. https://doi.org/10.18415/ijmmu.v7i6.1625.

Mualamat, N., Nurbaeti, I., & Palupi, P. (2020). The effectiveness of Dhikr to intensity of pain during active phase in mothers getting inducing labour. *Jurnal Keperawatan Padjadjaran, 8*(2), 183–190. https://repository.uinjkt.ac.id/dspace/bitstream/123456789/65723/1/Artikel%20The%20Effectiveness.pdf.

Musick, M. A., & Wilson, J. (2003). Volunteering and depression: The role of psychological and social resources in different age groups. *Social Science & Medicine (1982), 56*(2), 259–269. https://doi.org/10.1016/s0277-9536(02)00025-4.

Nasiri, S. (2010). The effect of listening to religious prayers on health outcomes in patients with chronic disease. *Iranian Journal of Spiritual Medicine, 25*(4), 233–239.

Newberg, A., Pourdehnad, M., Alavi, A., & d'Aquili, E. G. (2003). Cerebral blood flow during meditative prayer: Preliminary findings and methodological issues. *Perceptual and Motor Skills, 97*(2), 625–630. https://doi.org/10.2466/pms.2003.97.2.625.

Newberg, A. B., Wintering, N. A., Yaden, D. B., Waldman, M. R., Reddin, J., & Alavi, A. (2015). A case series study of the neurophysiological effects of altered states of mind during intense Islāmic prayer. *Journal of Physiology, Paris, 109*(4–6), 214–220. https://doi.org/10.1016/j.jphysparis.2015.08.001.

Nosrati, F., Ghobari-Bonab, B., Zandi, S., & Qorbani-Vanajemi, M. (2021). Effects of Dhikr (Repetition of Holy Names) on stress: A systematic review. *Journal of Pishachis' Dār dīn va salāmat, 7*(3), 157–171. https://doi.org/10.22037/jrrh.v7i3.27320.

Owens, J., Rassool, G. Hussein, Bernstein, J., Latif, S., & Aboul-Enein, B. (2023). Interventions using the Qur'an to promote mental health: A systematic scoping review. *Journal of Mental Health, 32*(4), 842–862. https://doi.org/10.1080/09638237.2023.2232449.

Post, S. G. (2005). Altruism, happiness, and health: It's good to be good. *International Journal of Behavioral Medicine, 12*(2), 66–77.

Purwanto, S., Anganti, N. N. R., & Yahman, S. A. (2022). Validity and effectiveness of dhikr breathing relaxation model therapy on insomnia disorders. *Indigenous: Jurnal Ilmiah Psikologi, 7*(2), 119–129.

Qidwai, W., Tabassum, R., Hanif, R., & Khan, F. H. (2009). Belief in prayers and its role in healing among family practice patients visiting a teaching hospital in Karachi, Pakistan. *Pakistan Journal of Medical Sciences, 25*(2), 182–189.

Qidwai, W., Tabassum, R., Hanif, R., & Khan, F. H. (2010). Belief in charity giving (sadqa) and its role in healing: Results of a survey conducted at a teaching hospital in Karachi, Pakistan. *Oman Medical Journal, 25*(2), 108–113. https://doi.org/10.5001/omj.2010.30.

Rahman, H., & Hussin, S. (2021). Case study of using Ruqyah complementary therapy on a British Muslim patient with cluster headache. *European Journal of Medical and Health Sciences, 3*(1), 5–7. www.ejmed.org.

Rahnama, P., et al. (2012). Religious beliefs and spiritual health in cancer patients. *Iranian Journal of Cancer Prevention, 5*(2), 94–101.

Raposa, E. B., Laws, H. B., & Ansell, E. B. (2016). Prosocial behavior mitigates the negative effects of stress in everyday life. *Clinical Psychological Science, 4*(4), 691–698.

Rassool, G. Hussein. (2019). *Evil eye, Jinn possession and mental health issues: An Islāmic perspective.* Routledge.

Sabbagh, M., et al. (2012). Prayer as a preventative measure in cognitive health: A study in northern Israel. *Alzheimer's & Dementia, 8*(3), 177–182.

Sadaf, M. (2024). *Status of brain during prayers: Scientific analysis.* https://aboutislam. net/muslim-issues/science-muslim-issues/status-brain-prayers-scientific-analysis/

Saskia, b., Alizah, P. N., & Hoirunisah, S. et al., (2022). The usefulness of Ruqyah prayer in everyday life. *Proceeding Conference on Da'wah And Communication Studies, 1*(1), 30–35. https://proceedings.dokicti.org/index.php/CDCS/index30.

Schjødt, U., Stødkilde-Jørgensen, H., Geertz, A. W., & Roepstorff, A. (2008). Rewarding prayers. *Neuroscience Letters, 443*(3), 165–168. https://doi.org/10.1016/j. neulet.2008.07.068.

Shuluddin, J. (2016). Effectiveness of Ruqyah Syar'iyyah on physical disease treatment in a RIAU province. *Jurnal Ushuluddin, 24*(2), 211–233.

Solman, H., & Mohamed, S. (2013). Effects of zikr meditation and jaw relaxation on postoperative pain, anxiety and physiologic response of patients undergoing abdominal surgery. *Journal of Biology, Agriculture and Healthcare, 3*(2), 23–38.

Syahri, A., Marlina, S., Rosaulina, M., Manik, M. H., Harigustian, Y., Pasambo, Y., & Putra, K. A. N. (2024). The effectiveness of psychological Dhikr therapy in improving the quality of life of cancer patients undergoing chemotherapy. *Jurnal Ilmiah Perawat Manado (Juiperdo), 12*, 187–198, https://doi.org/10.47718/jpd.v12i2.2524.

Upenieks, L. (2023). Unpacking the relationship between prayer and anxiety: A consideration of prayer types and expectations in the United States. *Journal of Religion and Health, 62*(3), 1810–1831. https://doi.org/10.1007/s10943-022-01708-0.

Wachholtz, A. B., & Pargament, K. I. (2005). Is spirituality a critical ingredient of meditation? Comparing the effects of spiritual meditation, secular meditation, and relaxation on spiritual, psychological, cardiac, and pain outcomes. *Journal of Behavioral Medicine, 28*(4), 369–384. https://doi.org/10.1007/s10865-005-9008-5.

Wallace, J. M., Jr, & Forman, T. A. (1998). Religion's role in promoting health and reducing risk among American youth. *Health Education & Behavior: The Official Publication of the Society for Public Health Education, 25*(6), 721–741. https://doi. org/10.1177/109019819802500604.

Wyatt, T. (2020). *Protective prayers for relief and protection.* https://yaqeeninstitute. org/read/paper/duas-for-relief-and-protection#ftnt4

6 Islāmic perspectives on storytelling

Introduction

Storytelling plays a vital role in Islāmic Integrated Narrative Therapy (IINT), functioning as a powerful therapeutic method for imparting life lessons and fostering emotional healing. By drawing on stories from the Qur'ān, hadīths, and the lives of the Prophets (عليهم السلام), IINT helps individuals engage with spiritual teachings that offer guidance in facing hardship, cultivating resilience, and maintaining patience and trust in Allāh during times of trial (Hassem et al., 2025). These narratives enable clients to reflect on their own struggles, find meaning in their experiences, and draw strength from the examples of those who endured similar challenges with unwavering faith. The Prophets (عليهم السلام), who encountered numerous hardships, serve as inspiring models in IINT, demonstrating constructive coping strategies and showing how faith and perseverance can empower individuals to manage their difficulties. Through a strengthened spiritual connection, the practice of patience, and the pursuit of guidance through prayer and contemplation, clients can use these sacred stories to enhance their emotional resilience. Unlike traditional narrative therapy, IINT adopts a more collaborative approach to storytelling. In IINT, both the client and the therapist actively engage in constructing the narrative. The therapist not only listens but also contributes meaningfully, drawing on spiritual and religious sources – particularly the stories of the Prophets (عليهم السلام) as well as Qur'ānic and hadīth teachings. This dual narration approach is a key feature of IINT, as it values the client's lived experiences while incorporating the therapist's religious and therapeutic insights. Through the inclusion of Islāmic stories and teachings, the therapist offers spiritual encouragement, moral direction, and a framework for understanding personal difficulties from a faith-centred perspective. This shared narrative process fosters a deeper connection to spiritual knowledge while also addressing the emotional and the psychospiritual needs of the client. The purpose of this chapter is to explore the function and significance of storytelling within the framework of IINT.

DOI: 10.4324/9781003584995-7

Historical context of storytelling

Storytelling has a rich and enduring legacy, deeply embedded in the cultural fabric of the Arabian Peninsula long before the emergence of Islām. In pre-Islāmic society, oral traditions were the primary mode of communication and education, particularly in a largely illiterate population. Poets, bards, and storytellers held esteemed positions within their communities, tasked with preserving tribal histories, genealogies, and collective wisdom. Among these traditions, the *qaṣīda,* a form of oral poetry, was especially prominent, often used to convey praise, critique, or lamentation (Stetkevych, 2010). These oral narratives not only entertained but also served as vital tools for passing down values and knowledge across generations (Herzog, 2012; Siddique & Hussain, 2016). With the advent of Islām, storytelling took on an even more significant role as a means of transmitting religious teachings, cultural values, and moral guidance. The early Islāmic period emphasised oral tradition, exemplified by the preservation of the Qur'ān through memorisation and recitation by the Prophet's companions (*Sahabah*). Prophet Muhammad (ﷺ) used storytelling as a powerful educational tool to convey the divine message and ethical principles revealed in the Qur'ān. The practice of oral recitation (*tajwīd*) became, and remains, a cornerstone of Islāmic learning, highlighting the enduring importance of oral transmission in preserving and disseminating sacred knowledge.

Storytelling in Islām has its roots in the Qur'ān and *hadīths,* with the stories of the Prophets (*Qisas al-Anbiya*) such as Prophet Adam, Prophet Nuh (Noah), Prophet Ibrahim (Abraham), Musa (Moses), and Yusuf (Joseph). The stories of the Prophets (عليهم السلام) and past communities were shared to provide guidance, cautionary tales, teach moral values like patience, faith, and justice, while also warning against vices, and reflections on human behaviour. Surah Yusuf (Chapter 12), for example, offers a detailed account of the life of Prophet Yusuf (عليهم السلام) and conveys moral lessons about trust, patience, and forgiveness. A verse from the Qur'ân highlights the storytelling nature of the scripture:

نَحْنُ نَقُصُّ عَلَيْكَ أَحْسَنَ ٱلْقَصَصِ بِمَآ أَوْحَيْنَآ إِلَيْكَ هَٰذَا ٱلْقُرْءَانَ وَإِن كُنتَ مِن قَبْلِهِ لَمِنَ ٱلْغَٰفِلِينَ

- *We relate to you, [O Muhammad], the best of stories in what We have revealed to you of this Qur'ān although you were, before it, among the unaware.* (Yusuf 12:3, interpretation of the meaning).

In his exegesis, Ibn 'Abbâs, explained that "(We narrate unto thee (Muhammad)) We clarify to you (the best of narratives) the best story of the news of Joseph and his brothers." (in that We have inspired in you) with which We inspired through Gabriel (this Qur'an) in this Qur'ān, (though aforetime) before Gabriel brought down the Qur'ān, to you (thou wast of the heedless) in relation to the event of Joseph and his brothers. *Hadīth* literature, like Sahih Bukhârî, Sahih Muslim and others (Sunnah.Com) contains numerous narrative-based teachings from the Prophet Muhammad (ﷺ) that impart ethical, moral, practical, and spiritual lessons.

As Islām expanded, religious scholars, Imams, and educators increasingly turned to storytelling as a means of addressing practical matters related to morality, ethics, and spirituality. The narrative traditions found in the Qur'ān and *hadīth* became essential for conveying moral, ethical, and social teachings. Sufi mystics further enriched this heritage, employing stories to communicate profound spiritual insights. Figures such as Rumi and Saadi used storytelling as a powerful medium to illustrate spiritual truths, Rumi's *Masnavi*, for instance, is filled with parables and allegories that continue to resonate with audiences worldwide, both Muslim and non-Muslim (Barks, 2004). Over time, Islāmic storytelling incorporated elements of local folklore and cultural traditions, embedding itself deeply into the social and cultural fabric of Muslim communities. These narratives, often centred on themes like justice, morality, and destiny, served not only to entertain but also to instill fundamental Islāmic values. In contemporary settings, storytelling remains a vital tool for education and therapeutic practices, continuing its legacy as a powerful means of guidance, reflection, and healing.

The storytelling tradition in Islām, deeply rooted in the Qur'ānic narratives of the Prophets and their moral teachings, serves as a powerful educational and spiritual tool. Stories of figures such as Prophets Ādam, Nūh, and Ibrāhīm (عليهم السلام) convey essential virtues like patience, faith, and justice, while also offering warnings against moral failings. These narratives help make complex theological ideas more relatable and understandable for a broad audience, preserving the rich cultural and spiritual heritage of the Islāmic world. Storytelling also nurtures spiritual development by inspiring faith, encouraging perseverance, and prompting individuals to reflect on their relationship with Allāh. On a communal level, it fosters unity, provides role models, and supports the transmission of Islāmic knowledge and values across generations. As noted by Abbasedu (2025), storytelling in the Islāmic tradition fulfills multiple functions: it demystifies complex religious concepts, safeguards cultural heritage, and promotes personal and spiritual growth. He further emphasises its role in strengthening community bonds, facilitating moral role modeling, and ensuring the continuity of Islāmic teachings through shared narratives and collective memory.

Storytelling in Qur'ân and hadīth

The Qur'ān serves as the cornerstone of Islāmic narratives (*qissah*) and storytelling. Described as "*a royal tapestry*" where each thread represents a divine revelation intricately woven into a masterpiece of spiritual insight, it offers both personal guidance and a framework for societal values (Religion24, 2025). The power of Qur'ānic storytelling lies in its timeless relevance, transcending historical, cultural, and religious boundaries to speak to the universal human experience. Its narratives explore themes such as faith, perseverance, justice, jealousy, and mercy, core aspects of the human condition, making them meaningful for individuals from all walks of life. Through parables, allegories, and historical accounts, the Qur'ān imparts profound lessons on ethical conduct, moral strength, and life's challenges. These stories encourage deep reflection, foster spiritual development, and promote virtues like compassion, patience, and resilience. Regardless of one's religious or cultural background, the wisdom embedded in Qur'ānic stories offers enduring guidance and inspiration for all humanity.

One of the most remarkable features of the Qur'ān is its distinctive narrative style, which is crafted to convey profound moral, ethical, and spiritual lessons. Each story invites the audience to engage in deep reflection, urging them to consider their own actions and life choices in light of the teachings presented. The Qur'ān employs a variety of narrative techniques to communicate these lessons. Some stories, like that of Prophet Yūsuf (عليه السلام) are told in a linear, chronological sequence, providing a complete and cohesive account. Others, such as the story of Mūsā, are revealed non-sequentially across multiple sūrahs (chapters), emphasising recurring themes and spiritual insights over linear progression. A unique feature of Qur'ānic storytelling is its use of direct address, speaking personally to the reader or listener to foster a sense of connection and immediacy. Dialogues between prophets and their communities add further depth, making the messages more relatable and emotionally resonant. The Qur'ān also employs symbolic parables, such as the parable of the good tree in Sūrah Ibrāhīm, to convey deep spiritual truths through metaphor. Moreover, the stories of past nations and their downfall serve as cautionary tales, warning against moral corruption and disobedience. By dispersing revelations across different sūrahs, the Qur'ān encourages *tadabbur* (deep reflection), prompting readers to think critically and draw broader lessons from the interconnected narratives.

Types, description, examples, and function of Qur'ânic narrative

The Qur'ān presents a diverse range of narratives, each serving multiple purposes. These include prophetic narratives, parabolic stories, historical accounts, as well as personal and communal narratives, alongside significant events from the life of Prophet Muhammad (ﷺ). Each of these narrative types highlights essential aspects of the Qur'ānic message and fulfills distinct roles within the broader context of Islāmic teachings. According to Von Denffer (2024), these narratives function in six key ways:

- Explaining the overall message of Islām
- Offering general guidance and reminders

- Strengthening the conviction of the Prophet and his followers
- Recalling the experiences and challenges of earlier prophets
- Demonstrating the continuity and truth of the Prophet Muhammad's message
- Providing responses to critics of Islām, including Jews and Christians

These six functions can be grouped under broader categories: guidance, reflection, emotional impact, spiritual enlightenment, moral instruction, and community building. While all six functions can be found across the different types of narratives, certain functions may be more prominent in specific categories. For example, community building may be particularly emphasised in prophetic or historical narratives, whereas emotional resonance and spiritual insight are present across all categories but may vary in depth and focus depending on the narrative's context and content.

The significant events in the life of Prophet Muhammad (ﷺ) are rich with timeless lessons that offer guidance, opportunities for reflection, and deep spiritual insight for believers. While many pivotal moments shaped his life and mission, the following events stand out for their profound impact and the valuable teachings they impart. The *Hijrah* (migration to Madinah) embodies lessons in trust in Allāh, patience during hardship, and the importance of unity within the Muslim community. It also marked the establishment of the first Islāmic state. The Night Journey (*Isrā'* and *Mi'rāj*) deepened the understanding of spiritual proximity to Allāh, offering a powerful example of the unseen dimensions of faith. The Battle of Badr illustrated how unwavering belief can prevail despite overwhelming odds, while the Battles of Uhud and Al-Ahzāb emphasised the need for unity, discipline, and resilience in the face of adversity. The Treaty of Hudaybiyyah highlighted the value of wisdom, diplomacy, and long-term vision in leadership and conflict resolution. The Conquest of Makkah exemplifies the victory of truth through strategic patience, compassion, and forgiveness. Finally, the Farewell Sermon captured the Prophet's (ﷺ) final counsel to the *Ummah*, underscoring principles of justice, equality, and mutual care. Collectively, these events reinforce the conviction of believers and serve as enduring sources of guidance, spiritual awakening, moral instruction, and the strengthening of community bonds.

Prophetic narratives in Islām convey profound moral and spiritual teachings through the trials and triumphs of Prophets such as Ādam, Nūḥ, Ibrāhīm, Yūsuf, and Mūsā (عليهم السلام). These stories highlight essential virtues like faith, patience, and justice, offering guidance for navigating life's difficulties with trust in Allāh. They encourage self-reflection, stir emotional resonance, and inspire spiritual growth, reinforcing values such as humility, forgiveness, and integrity, while fostering unity within the Muslim *Ummah*. Parabolic narratives, also referred to as allegorical or metaphorical stories, communicate deep spiritual and ethical lessons through symbolic language. For example, the parable of the good and bad tree in Sūrah Ibrāhīm (14:24–26) illustrates the strength of faith and the lasting impact of righteous deeds. Similarly, the image of the spider's web in Sūrah Al-'Ankabūt (29:41) symbolises the weakness of relying on anything other than God. These brief yet powerful metaphors convey insights into the nature of good and evil, the consequences of human choices, and the necessity of spiritual awareness. Historical narratives, by contrast, focus on the rise and decline of past civilisations, such as the peoples of 'Ād and Thamūd, as warnings to future generations. These accounts emphasise the dangers of arrogance, injustice, and the rejection of divine truth, urging believers to reflect on history and learn from the mistakes of those who came before.

Hereafter narratives in the Qur'ān depict the destinies of the righteous and the wicked in the afterlife, emphasising themes of accountability, reward, and punishment. These stories, including vivid descriptions of the Day of Judgement and the account of the People of the Garden (*Ashāb al-Jannah*), encourage reflection on the fleeting nature of worldly life and the enduring reality of the Hereafter. In addition, personal and community narratives illustrate the experiences of individuals and groups, often highlighting their struggles with faith and the role of divine intervention in their lives. Examples such as the story of Maryam (عليهم السلام) and the birth of 'Īsā (عليهم السلام), or the account of Prophet Yūsuf (عليهم السلام), provide practical guidance and moral lessons while stressing the importance of community strength and shared faith during challenging times.

Together, these varied narrative forms within Islām offer a holistic understanding of human experience and deliver profound insights into faith, morality, and the divine. Table 6.1 summarises the different types of narratives and their functions in Qur'ānic storytelling.

Allegories, real-life events, metaphors, and parables are related but distinct storytelling techniques. Table 6.2 presents the key techniques in Qur'ânic narratives.

Stories and lessons from *hadīths*

The *hadīth*, also known as *al-Riwayāt*, are the recorded sayings and actions of Prophet Muhammad (ﷺ), offering deep insight into his life, character, and teachings. Complementing the Qur'ān, these narrations serve as an important source of guidance for Muslims, providing both practical advice and spiritual wisdom for everyday life. *Hadīth* stories convey the Prophet's teachings in a relatable and accessible way, highlighting core values such as patience, justice, compassion, and sincerity. These principles make *hadīth* particularly valuable in the context of IINT, where they can be used to help individuals reframe their personal narratives within an Islāmic worldview. In therapeutic settings, *hadīth* serve as moral and spiritual anchors, assisting clients in finding meaning in their challenges and fostering resilience. For example, the Prophet (ﷺ) frequently emphasised *sabr* (patience) in the face of adversity, a theme that aligns closely with therapeutic approaches that encourage individuals to reinterpret difficulties as opportunities for growth, healing, and deeper spiritual connection.

Table 6.1 Narrative types and functions of Qur'ānic storytelling

Type	Description	Examples	Functions¹
Significant events Prophet Muhammad (ﷺ)	Key events from the life of Prophet Muhammad (ﷺ) that offer guidance and lessons.	The Hijrah (Migration to Medina (AtTawbah 9:40). The Night Journey (Al Isra' 17:1). The Battle of Badr (Al 'Imran 3:13); Uhud (Al Imran 3:121–128; Al-Ahzab 33:9–27). The Treaty of Hudaybiyyah (Al Fath 48:1). The Conquest of Mecca (Nasr 110:1). The Farewell Sermon – (Al-Ma'idah 5:3).	Guidance, Reflection, Emotional impact, Spiritual enlightenment, Moral teaching, Community building
Prophetic narratives	Stories of prophets and their communities for moral and spiritual lessons.	Prophet Adam (AS) – Creation and fall (Al-Baqarah 2:30–38). Prophet Noah (AS) – The flood (Hud 11:25–48). Prophet Moses (AS) – Confrontation with Pharaoh (Al-Qasas 28:3–46).	Guidance, Reflection, Emotional impact, Spiritual enlightenment, Moral teaching, Community building
Parabolic narratives	Allegories and metaphors illustrating moral and spiritual truths.	Good and bad tree (Ibrahim 14:24–26). Spider's web (Al-Ankabut 29:41). Dead land revived by rain (Al-Hajj 22:5).	Guidance, Reflection, Emotional impact, Spiritual enlightenment, Moral teaching
Historical narratives	Stories of past civilisations and their rise or fall as lessons for humanity.	People of 'Aad and Thamud (Al-Fajr 89:6–13). People of the cave (Ashab al-Kahf) (Al-Kahf 18:9–26). Dhul-Qarnayn's journey (Al-Kahf 18:83–98).	Guidance, Reflection, Emotional impact, Spiritual enlightenment, Moral teaching, Community building
Hereafter narratives	Descriptions of the Hereafter, Paradise, and Hell to instill faith and accountability	Story of the People of the Garden (Ashab al-Jannah) (Al-Qalam 68:17–33). Day of resurrection (Al-Waqi'ah 56:1–56). Scenes from Day of Judgement (Abasa 80:33–42). The Fate of the righteous (Al-Insān 76:5–22) and the wicked (Al-Insan 76: 3-4).	Guidance, Reflection, Emotional impact, Spiritual enlightenment, Moral teaching
Personal and community narratives	Stories of individuals or groups showing trials, faith, and divine intervention.	Story of Maryam (AS*) and the Birth of Isa (AS) (Maryam 19:16–36). Story of Qarun (Korah) and His Wealth (Al-Qasas 28:76–82). -Story of Prophet Yusuf (AS) (Yusuf 12).	Guidance, Reflection, Emotional impact, Spiritual enlightenment, Moral teaching

*AS- (عليه السلام)

Table 6.2 Key techniques in Qur'ânic narrative

Technique	Definition	Example from the Qur'an	Key features
Allegories	Extended symbolic stories. where characters and events represent deeper moral, spiritual, or philosophical meanings.	The story of the People of the Cave (Al-Kahf 18:9–26) – Symbolising faith and perseverance.	A complete narrative with symbolic meaning beyond the literal story.
Real-life events	Factual. Convey divine wisdom and moral lessons.	The Battle of Badr (Al-Imran 3:13) – A real event with lessons on faith, strategy, and divine support.	Based on factual events, providing historical and moral insights.
Metaphors	Direct symbolic comparisons used to explain abstract ideas.	"Allah is the Light of the heavens and the earth" (An-Nur 24:35), Light represents divine guidance.	A single comparison illustrating a deeper truth.
Parables	Short, self-contained moral lessons.	The parable of the good and bad tree (Ibrahim 14:24–26), Representing the consequences of good and evil actions.	Brief, self-contained narratives delivering a clear moral lesson.

The Prophet Muhammad (ﷺ) acknowledged and addressed psychological challenges, setting a precedent for future generations of Muslims to recognise and manage their emotional and mental well-being. Although the prophets were the most noble of humanity, they too experienced profound emotions such as grief, sorrow, and anxiety (Awaad, 2020). Islām encourages believers to seek appropriate treatment for mental health concerns such as anxiety, worry, and fear by consulting qualified professionals. In a *hadīth* narrated by Usāmah ibn Sharīk (may Allāh be pleased with him), he recounts:

> I came to the Prophet (ﷺ) while his Companions sat around him so still it was as if birds were perched on their heads. I greeted him and sat down. Then desert Arabs arrived from various directions and asked, "O Messenger of Allāh, should we seek medical treatment?" He replied, "Yes, seek medical treatment, for Allāh has not created a disease without also creating its remedy, except for on, old age."

> (Abū Dāwūd (a))

This guidance emphasises that suffering in silence can hinder recovery, while seeking help is a responsible and encouraged step towards healing. Islām advocates for taking action to ease one's difficulties while maintaining trust in Allāh. Pursuing treatment, whether for physical ailments or emotional and psychological struggles, is a way of utilising the knowledge and resources that Allāh has made available. True strength lies not in enduring hardship alone but in recognising the need for support and taking steps towards improvement. As reported by Abū al-Dardā', the Prophet (ﷺ) said: "Allāh has sent down both the disease and the cure, and He has appointed a remedy for every illness, so treat yourselves medically, but do not use anything unlawful" (Abū Dāwūd (b)).

In Islām, suffering is not viewed as meaningless or purely negative. Instead, it is often seen as a test, a means of spiritual purification, and an opportunity for personal and spiritual growth. It is narrated by Abū Sa'īd al-Khudrī and Abū Hurayrah that the Prophet Muhammad (ﷺ) said: "No fatigue, nor disease, nor sorrow, nor sadness, nor hurt, nor distress befalls a Muslim, even the prick of a thorn, except that Allāh expiates some of his sins because of it" (Bukhārī). While suffering can be difficult to endure, Islāmic teachings emphasise that it holds hidden blessings. It serves as a form of cleansing from sin, a test of one's faith, a source of spiritual elevation, and a means of attaining Allāh's mercy and reward. Those who face hardship with patience and gratitude are promised a higher status in the sight of Allāh. Abū Sa'īd al-Khudrī also reported:

> I visited the Prophet (ﷺ) when he was suffering from a fever. I placed my hand on him and felt its heat through the blanket. I said, "O Messenger of Allāh, how intense is your suffering!" He replied, "We Prophets are tested more severely, and so our reward is greater." I asked, "O Messenger of Allāh, who are tested most severely?" He said, "The Prophets." I asked, "Then who?" He said, "Then the righteous. Some are tested with such poverty that they have nothing but a cloak to wrap around themselves. Yet one of them would rejoice in hardship as you rejoice in ease."
>
> (Ibn Mājah (a))

These teachings highlight that trials are not punishments but opportunities for spiritual refinement, deeper faith, and closeness to Allāh.

The following *hadīth* illustrates that hardships, while difficult, can be viewed as opportunities for spiritual growth and divine reward. Recognising the temporary nature of grief helps believers maintain emotional balance during trying times, nurturing *sabr* (patience) and *tawakkul* (trust in Allāh). It is narrated from Umm Salamah that her husband, Abū Salamah, once told her he heard the Messenger of Allāh (ﷺ) say:

> No Muslim is afflicted with a calamity and responds by saying what Allāh has commanded: "*Innā lillāhi wa innā ilayhi rāji'ūn. Allāhumma 'indaka*

aḥtasabtu muṣībatī, fa-ajurnī fīhā, wa ʿawwiḍnī minhā" (Truly, to Allāh we belong and truly, to Him we shall return. O Allāh, I seek reward from You for this calamity, so reward me for it and grant me something better in its place), except that Allāh will reward them and replace their loss with something better.

Umm Salamah continued:

When Abū Salamah passed away, I remembered his words and said: "*Innā lillāhi wa innā ilayhi rājiʿūn. Allāhumma ʿindaka aḥtasabtu muṣībatī, fa-ajurnī ʿalayhā.*" But when I came to say, "*wa ʿawwiḍnī minhā,*" I hesitated, thinking, "Who could be better than Abū Salamah?" Still, I said it, and Allāh rewarded me with Muhammad (ﷺ) as my husband.

(Ibn Mājah (b))

This powerful narration teaches believers to respond to hardship with faith and hope, trusting that Allāh's compensation is always better, even if it is not immediately apparent. Similarly, on the authority of ʿAbdullāh ibn ʿAbbās (may Allāh be pleased with him), the Prophet (ﷺ) said: "Know that victory comes with patience, relief with affliction, and ease with hardship" (An-Nawawī). This statement reinforces the concept that resilience and patience are essential in overcoming difficulties and cultivating emotional strength. Furthermore, suffering is not without merit. As narrated by Abū Hurayrah, the Prophet (ﷺ) said: "If Allāh wants good for someone, He puts them through trials" (Bukhārī (b)). Hardship, then, can be a sign of divine favour, offering hidden benefits and spiritual elevation. In moments of personal distress, the Prophet (ﷺ) would turn to prayer for comfort and strength. He would say to Bilāl (may Allāh be pleased with him): "Bilāl, bring us relief and comfort through the prayer (ṣalāh)" (Umm Umar Khaled, 2018). This reflects the Prophet's deep reliance on spiritual practices to cope with life's difficulties and his example encourages believers to do the same, finding peace, stability, and healing in their connection with Allāh.

The following hadīth highlights the Prophet Muhammad's (ﷺ) profound emotional depth and compassion. His grief over the death of his son Ibrāhīm reflects not only his deep love but also his humanity, affirming that expressing sorrow is entirely natural and fully aligned with Islāmic teachings. Anas ibn Mālik narrated:

We accompanied the Messenger of Allāh (ﷺ) to the blacksmith Abū Saif, the husband of the wet nurse of Ibrāhīm (the Prophet's son). The Prophet (ﷺ) took Ibrāhīm, kissed him, and smelled him. Later, we entered Abū Saif's home, where Ibrāhīm was taking his final breaths. The Prophet's (ﷺ)

eyes began to fill with tears. ʿAbdur Raḥmān ibn ʿAwf said, "O Messenger of Allāh, even you are weeping?" He replied, "O Ibn ʿAwf, this is mercy." Then he continued to weep and said, "The eyes shed tears, the heart feels sorrow, but we say only what pleases our Lord. O Ibrāhīm, indeed we are deeply grieved by your departure."

(Bukhārī (c))

This moment teaches the importance of embracing and acknowledging our emotions. Islām does not suppress natural feelings of grief; rather, it recognises them as part of the human experience. However, it encourages that mourning be observed within the boundaries of *ṣabr* (patience) and submission to Allāh's will. Even in pain, believers are guided to speak words that reflect faith and avoid expressions of despair or objection to Allāh's decree. The Prophet (ﷺ) also offered practical guidance for managing emotions in various situations. Abū Dharr reported: *"The Messenger of Allāh (ﷺ) said: If one of you becomes angry while standing, he should sit down. If the anger subsides, that is good. If not, he should lie down."* (Abū Dāwūd (c)). In another narration, Sulaimān ibn Surad reported:

Two men began insulting one another in the presence of the Prophet (ﷺ) while we were sitting with him. One of them became visibly angry, his face turning red. The Prophet (ﷺ) said, "I know a phrase which, if he were to say it, his anger would go away: *A ʿūdhu billāhi min al-shayṭān al-rajīm* (I seek refuge in Allāh from the accursed devil)."

(Bukhārī and Muslim)

Together, these teachings emphasise that Islām acknowledges emotional expression, while also providing guidance on how to manage emotions constructively and in a way that maintains spiritual and psychological balance.

The hadīth regarding *talbīnah,* a dish made from barley, demonstrates the therapeutic value of physical remedies in supporting emotional well-being. It is narrated by ʿUrwah that ʿĀʾishah (may Allāh be pleased with her) used to recommend *talbīnah* to those who were ill or grieving the loss of a loved one. She said: "I heard the Messenger of Allāh (ﷺ) say, '*Talbīnah* soothes the heart of the sick person and relieves some of their sorrow and grief'" (Bukhārī (d)). This narration highlights the connection between physical and emotional health, emphasising that nourishment and diet can influence mental and emotional states. In Islāmic tradition, the body and soul are deeply interconnected; caring for one can positively impact the other. Just as spiritual practices like *ṣalāh* (prayer) and *dhikr* (remembrance of Allāh) help ease emotional distress, physical measures, such as proper nutrition, rest, and medical care – are also important in alleviating psychological suffering. Furthermore, emotional well-being is closely tied to spiritual trust. 'Umar ibn al-Khaṭṭāb (may Allāh be pleased with him) reported that the Prophet (ﷺ) said: *"If you were to rely upon Allāh with true reliance, He would provide for you as He provides for the birds: they leave in the morning hungry and return in the evening full"* (Ibn Mājah (c)). This teaching reminds believers that placing sincere trust in Allāh brings peace of mind and eases anxiety. By surrendering to His will and trusting in His provision, one can navigate life's challenges with a calm heart, free from excessive worry and fear.

IINT draws on *hadīths* to support individuals in externalising their struggles and reshaping their personal narratives in accordance with Islāmic values. Sayings of the Prophet (ﷺ) concerning justice and sincerity, for example, provide a framework for resolving inner turmoil and guiding ethical decision-making. Stories that highlight the Prophet's mercy and forgiveness serve as powerful therapeutic tools, encouraging healing from trauma, nurturing self-compassion, and fostering reconciliation in relationships. This approach helps facilitate personal growth and spiritual transformation.

Table 6.3 outlines selected key *ahādīth* and their therapeutic relevance within the context of Islāmic Integrated Narrative Therapy.

Table 6.3 Summarising selected *hadīth* and their relevance to Islāmic Integrative Narrative Therapy

Theme	Hadīth *narration*	Application in Islāmically Modified Narrative Therapy
Patience *(sabr)* & resilience	"No fatigue, nor disease, nor sorrow, nor sadness, nor hurt, nor distress befalls a Muslim… but that Allāh expiates some of his sins for that" (Bukhârî (a)).	Helps clients reframe suffering as a means of purification and personal growth. Encourages endurance and patience in the face of challenges.
Seeking treatment & mental well-being	"Make use of medical treatment, for Allāh has not made a disease without appointing a remedy for it, with the exception of old age" (Abū Dāwūd).	Encourages individuals to seek professional help for psychological distress while maintaining faith in divine wisdom.
Suffering as spiritual growth	"If Allāh wants to do good to somebody, He afflicts him with trials" (Bukhârî (b)).	Reframes hardships as spiritual tests that lead to personal and faith-based development.

(Continued)

Table 6.3 (Continued)

Theme	Hadīth *narration*	Application in Islāmically Modified Narrative Therapy
Trust in Allāh (*tawakkul*)	"If you were to rely upon Allāh with the reliance He is due, you would be given provision like the birds: They go out hungry in the morning and come back with full bellies in the evening" (Ibn Majah).	Helps clients develop a mindset of trust and surrender to Allāh's plan, reducing anxiety and excessive worry.
Managing anger & emotional regulation	"When one of you becomes angry while standing, he should sit down. If the anger leaves him, well and good; otherwise, he should lie down" (Abū Dāwūd).	Provides practical strategies for emotional regulation and anger management in therapeutic settings.
Healing through diet & nutrition	"At-*Talbeena* gives rest to the heart of the patient and makes it active and relieves some of his sorrow and grief" (Bukhârî (d)).	Recognises the link between physical and emotional health; promotes holistic well-being.
Grief & mourning with faith	"The eyes are shedding tears, and the heart is grieved, and we will not say except what pleases our Lord, O Ibrahim! Indeed, we are grieved by your separation" (Bukhârî (c)).	Encourages healthy emotional expression, balancing grief with faith in divine wisdom.
Coping with loss & finding meaning	"There is no Muslim who is stricken with a calamity and reacts by saying… 'O Allāh, with You I seek reward for my calamity, so reward me for it and compensate me,' but Allāh will reward him for that and compensate him with something better" (Ibn Majah).	Assists clients in reframing loss and grief, fostering resilience and hope through faith.
Mercy & forgiveness in trauma recovery	"Bilal, bring us comfort and relief through *salah* (prayer)" (Umm Umar Khaled, 2018).	Encourages clients to find solace in prayer and spiritual connection during emotional distress.
Seeking treatment	"God has sent down both the disease and the cure, and He has appointed a cure for every disease, so treat yourselves medically, but use nothing unlawful" (Abū Dāwūd).	Helps clients to seek treatments that are permissible (*halāl*) and avoid those that contradict Islāmic principles.

The therapeutic value of Qur'ânic stories

Storytelling has long been recognised as a powerful psychological tool for healing and personal transformation. In the context of IINT, stories from the Qur'ān and *hadīth* provide individuals with relatable examples of struggle, perseverance, and divine guidance, fostering empathy, connection, and a sense of shared humanity. By reflecting on the trials faced by Prophets and the righteous, individuals are encouraged to reframe their own challenges in a more hopeful and constructive way, reducing feelings of isolation and despair. Furthermore, these sacred narratives support cognitive and moral development by offering clear ethical teachings that help guide individuals towards wiser, values-based decision-making. Through thoughtful reflection (*tadabbur*), clients develop greater self-awareness and deeper understanding of their emotions, thoughts, and behaviours. This process allows them to realign their personal stories with Islāmic principles and spiritual purpose, supporting not only emotional healing but also meaningful, faith-anchored growth.

In addition to their psychological value, Islāmically rooted narratives provide profound spiritual enrichment, deepening one's connection with Allāh and reinforcing faith. Stories from the lives of the Prophets, righteous individuals, and others serve as reminders that life's trials are purposeful, designed as opportunities for resilience, personal growth, and spiritual elevation. These narratives offer comfort and hope during times of hardship, reassuring believers that Allāh's mercy, wisdom, and plan encompass every challenge. Moreover, the moral and ethical teachings embedded in these stories inspire individuals to embody values such as patience (*ṣabr*), gratitude (*shukr*), and trust in Allāh (*tawakkul*). By internalising and applying these principles, individuals not only enhance their spiritual well-being but also foster inner peace and emotional stability. This grounded spiritual perspective helps reduce anxiety and distress, empowering believers to navigate life with clarity, faith, and balance.

Conclusion

In conclusion, Islāmic storytelling serves as a therapeutic tool that bridges psychological well-being and spiritual development. By drawing upon the lessons found in Qur'ānic narratives and *hadīth*, individuals can process their struggles with a renewed sense of purpose, resilience, and faith. Islāmic stories not only offer guidance on navigating life's challenges but also instil a sense of hope, reinforcing that hardship is often accompanied by ease. When incorporated into therapy, these narratives help individuals reshape their personal stories in a way that aligns with their faith, fostering both psychological healing and spiritual empowerment.

References

Abbasedu, M. (2025). *The role of storytelling in Islāmic tradition*. https://fiveable.me/the-islamic-world/unit-8/islamic-storytelling-traditions/study-guide/pssGdalqEabD7iDj

Abū Dāwūd (a). *Sunan Abū Dāwūd 3855*. In-book reference: Book 29, Hadīth 1. English translation: Book 28, Hadīth 3846. Sahih (Al-Albani). https://sunnah.com/abudawud: 3855.

Abū Dāwūd (b). *Mishkat al-Masabih 4538*.In-book reference: Book 23, Hadīth 25. https://sunnah.com/mishkat:4538.

Abū Dāwūd (c). *Sunan Abi Dawud 4782*. In-book reference: Book 43, Hadīth 10. English translation: Book 42, Hadīth 476. Sahih (Al-Albani). https://sunnah.com/abudawud:4782.

An Nawawi. *Hadīth 19, 40* Hadīth an-Nawawi. https://sunnah.com/nawawi40:19.

Awaad, R. (2020). *Prophet Muhammad's approach to mental health | Holistic healing* Yaqeen Institute Stanford Muslim Mental Health Laboratory. https://www.youtube.com/watch?v=fbD-Cez4EQU

Barks, C. (2004). *Rumi (Jalāl ad-Dīn Muḥammad Balkhī). The essential Rumi.* HarperOne.

Bukhârî (a). *Sahih al-Bukhârî 5641, 5642*. In-book reference: Book 75, Hadīth 2. USC-MSA web (English) reference: Vol. 7, Book 70, Hadīth 545. https://sunnah.com/bukhari:5641.

Bukhârî (b). *Sahih al-Bukhârî 5645*. In-book reference: Book 75, Hadīth 5. USC-MSA web (English) reference: Vol. 7, Book 70, Hadīth 548. https://sunnah.com/bukhari:5645.

Bukhârî (c). *Sahih al-Bukhârî 1303*. In-book reference: Book 23, Hadīth 61. USC-MSA web (English) reference: Vol. 2, Book 23, Hadīth 390. https://sunnah.com/bukhari:1303.

Bukhârî (d). *Sahih al-Bukhârî 5689*. In-book reference: Book 76, Hadīth 12. USC-MSA web (English) reference: Vol. 7, Book 71, Hadīth 593. https://sunnah.com/bukhari:5689.

Hassem, Z., Ismail, S., Vad Walla, N., & Rassool, G. H. (2025). *Working with crisis and trauma from an Islāmic perspective* (1st ed.). Routledge. https://doi.org/10.4324/9781003400295

Herzog, T. (2012). Orality and the tradition of Arabic epic storytelling. In K. Reichl (Ed.), *Medieval oral literature* (pp. 629–652). De Gruyter.

Ibn 'Abbâs. *Tanwir al-Miqbâs min Tafsîr Ibn 'Abbâs*. https://surahquran.com/tafsir-english.php?sora=12&aya=3.

Ibn Majah (a). *Sunan Ibn Majah 4024*. In-book reference: Book 36, Hadīth 99. English translation: Vol. 5, Book 36, Hadīth 4024. Hasan (Darussalam) https://sunnah.com/ibnmajah:4024.

Ibn Majah (b). *Sunan Ibn Majah 1598*. In-book reference: Book 6, Hadīth 166. English translation: Vol. 1, Book 6, Hadīth 1598. Hasan (Darussalam https://sunnah.com/ibnmajah:1598.

Ibn Majah (c). *Sunan Ibn Majah 4164*. In-book reference: Book 37, Hadīth 65. English translation: Vol. 5, Book 37, Hadīth 4164. Hasan (Darussalam). https://sunnah.com/ibnmajah:4164#:~:text=%E2%80%9CI%20heard%20the%20Messenger%20of%20Allāh%20%28%EF%B7%BA%29%20say%3A,come%20back%20with%20full%20bellies%20in%20the%20evening.%E2%80%9D

Religion24. (2025). *The power of storytelling in Islām: A comprehensive guide.* https://religion24.net/what-is-the-role-of-storytelling-in-Islām /:~:text=Delve%20into%20the%20rich%20tapestry%20of%20storytelling%20in,tools%20for%20teaching%2C%20inspiring%2C%20and%20preserving%20Islāmic %20values

Siddique, A. S., & Hussain, M. (2016). Pre-Islāmic Arabic prose literature & its growth. *International Education and Research Journal, 2*(1), 103–104.

Stetkevych, S. P. (2010). From Jāhiliyyah to Badīciyyah: Orality, literacy, and the transformations of rhetoric in Arabic poetry. *Oral Tradition, 25*(1), 211–230.

Sunnah.Com. *The Hadīth of the Prophet Muhammad* (صلى الله عليه و سلم) *at your finger-tips.* https://sunnah.com/.

Umm Umar Khaled. (2018). Stories of the Sahabah. Cited from *the Nafs Book*, Umm Umar Khaled, (pp. 152–153). https://storiesofthesahabah.tumblr.com/post/161547986751/do-you-miss-the-prophet-%EF%B7%BA-have-you-ever-felt.

Von Denffer, A. (2024). *6 patterns of narratives in the Quran.*

7 Use of metaphor in Islāmic Integrated Narrative Therapy

Introduction

Metaphors (أمثلة) serve as a key point of convergence between narrative therapy and Islāmic traditions, playing a vital role in IINT. These figurative expressions offer a powerful means of communication, enabling individuals to articulate abstract or complex emotional experiences in more tangible ways. Defined as "a figure of speech in which a word or phrase literally denoting one kind of object or idea is used in place of another to suggest a likeness or analogy between them" (www.merriam-webster.com), metaphors facilitate deeper insight, reflection, and personal growth by bridging the gap between thoughts and emotions. Metaphors are naturally embedded in everyday language, often emerging spontaneously in therapy sessions (Törneke, 2017). They are particularly prominent when clients describe intense emotional experiences, offering a valuable tool for expressing feelings that may be difficult to communicate directly (Fainsilber & Ortony, 1987; Wickman et al., 1999). This makes it essential for therapists to identify and engage with metaphors meaningfully during sessions. Numerous metaphor collections tailored to various client issues are presented in the literature (Killick et al., 2016).

Metaphors are especially effective in revealing the client's worldview and the underlying stories shaping their identity. Incorporating metaphors into therapy enriches the process, making it more dynamic and personally meaningful (Malkomsen et al., 2022).

In IINT, metaphors help clients externalise their problems, providing alternative perspectives and allowing them to construct more empowering personal narratives. The narrative metaphor framework highlights that individuals are active storytellers of their lives, and metaphors can help reshape those stories in more constructive ways. Sue et al. (2022) highlight the effectiveness of using metaphoric statements and storytelling in therapy, as these approaches enable clients to form personal and unique mental images that support their healing process. Similarly, Witztum et al. (1988, p. 2) propose that when therapists use metaphoric language and narratives, they implicitly communicate therapeutic strategies. These stories subtly suggest courses of action, which, when the client

DOI: 10.4324/9781003584995-8

follows through, can lead to the resolution of their psychological challenges. The aim of this chapter is to explore the role and therapeutic value of metaphor within the framework of Islāmic Modified Narrative Therapy.

Client-generated and therapist-generated metaphors

The use of metaphors in therapy is a collaborative process, co-created by both therapist and client (Wagener, 2017), and shaped by the client's individual experiences and cultural context. This perspective challenges the traditional notion that metaphors are solely generated by the therapist, instead highlighting the shared creation of meaning that strengthens the therapeutic alliance (Lloyd, 2017; Mathieson et al., 2015). Client-generated metaphors, phrases used by clients to express their emotions, experiences, or perceptions, offer valuable insight into their internal world. In therapeutic work with Muslim clients, these metaphors are often deeply influenced by their cultural and religious heritage. For instance, a client might say, "I feel like I'm carrying the world on my shoulders," a metaphor that vividly conveys the emotional weight of overwhelming responsibilities and obligations.

Therapist-generated metaphors play a key role in helping clients move towards their therapeutic goals. When therapists introduce metaphors that resonate with a client's lived experiences, they can clarify complex emotions or situations, making them more comprehensible and easier to engage with (Wagener, 2017). This method enhances insight and empowers clients to approach their challenges with greater clarity and confidence. For example, a therapist might use the metaphor *"Planting seeds of patience"*: cultivating patience is like planting a seed in fertile soil. With consistent care, through water, sunlight, and protection, the seed gradually grows into a strong tree that eventually bears fruit. In the same way, nurturing patience with continuous effort and trust in Allāh's divine timing fosters resilience and spiritual growth. This metaphor reflects how the development of virtues, like plants, requires time, attention, and faith. Although therapist-generated metaphors can be effective, research suggests that client-generated metaphors offer distinct advantages. Clients tend to connect more deeply with their own metaphors, leading to a stronger therapeutic alliance, increased cultural relevance, and more impactful cognitive and emotional shifts. Moreover, these metaphors are often more memorable than those introduced by the therapist (Angus & Greenberg, 2011; Angus & Rennie, 1988; Kopp, 1995; Lyddon et al., 2001; Martin et al., 1992; Witztum et al., 1988).

However, it is important for therapists to ensure that the metaphors used are culturally sensitive and align with the client's spirituality, cultural context, and personal experiences. Misaligned metaphors can lead to misunderstandings or disengagement. Therefore, effective therapist-generated metaphors should be collaboratively developed, taking into account the client's unique context and worldview.

Qur'ânic metaphors and Islāmic Integrated Narrative Therapy

In Islāmic traditions, metaphors are prevalent in the Qur'ân, conveying profound spiritual and moral concepts. Metaphors in the Qur'ân serve to capture complex ideas, make them more accessible, and stimulate deeper contemplation (*tafakkur and tadabbur*). Integrating Qur'ānic metaphors and analogies into therapeutic sessions can be highly effective when working with Muslim clients. Armstrong and Munro (2018) suggest that "adherent Muslims have a natural metaphorical way of thinking that connects with some of the post-structural therapeutic skills and techniques and at the same time draw on past Qur'ānic solutions for contemporary problems" (p. 174). This approach offers several benefits:

- Shared Islāmic worldview: Islāmic psychotherapists and their Muslim clients often share a common faith-based perspective, facilitating a deeper therapeutic connection.
- Receptiveness to Qur'ānic teachings: Muslim clients typically find comfort and guidance in Qur'ānic verses and Islāmic principles, viewing them as sources of solace during challenging times (Ahammed, 2010).
- Familiarity with Qur'ānic metaphors: Many Muslim clients are acquainted with the metaphors and parables found in the Qur'ān, enabling them to relate these analogies to their personal experiences.
- Integration into daily life: Some Muslim clients naturally incorporate Qur'ānic metaphors into everyday conversations, reflecting the deep integration of these concepts into their worldview.

By weaving Qur'ānic metaphors into the therapeutic process, therapists can create a culturally and spiritually resonant environment that aligns with the client's beliefs and values, thereby enhancing the effectiveness of therapy.

Islāmic psychotherapists can incorporate "metaphor therapy" techniques (Ahammed, 2010) into IINT to address deep existential concerns, reinforce clients' faith in Allāh, and offer culturally meaningful responses to modern challenges. Qur'ānic metaphors, in particular, hold great therapeutic value within an Islāmic framework. They can be used to encourage cycles of reflection and contemplation, promote insight, foster emotional expression, and enhance hope and resilience. These metaphors convey profound spiritual truths and help bridge the communication gap between therapist and client, creating a shared symbolic language for understanding experiences and navigating difficulties. Besides, they offer a meaningful structure through which clients can interpret their emotional psychological and spiritual struggles. Suhadi (2011) stresses that an Islāmic psychotherapist using a narrative approach must be well versed in the Qur'ān and its *tafsīr* (exegesis), while remaining within the boundaries of their professional competence and ethical practice.

Qur'ânic metaphors

The Qur'ân employs a wide range of metaphors to convey deep spiritual and ethical teachings through vivid and relatable imagery. These metaphors simplify complex ideas, encouraging believers to contemplate the realities of life, their connection with Allāh, and the path to righteous living. Within IINT, such metaphors serve a powerful therapeutic function. When drawn from the Qur'ân and Islāmic tradition, they resonate deeply with clients' spiritual beliefs, enhancing the relevance and effectiveness of the therapeutic experience.

The Qur'ān employs vivid metaphors to communicate profound spiritual insights that also align with key psychological concepts. One powerful example is the metaphor of the "good word as a good tree" (Ibrahim, 14:24), where righteous speech and action are likened to a tree with deep roots and branches reaching the sky. This imagery symbolises the strength, growth, and spiritual elevation of a believer whose consistent good deeds bear a lasting impact. Psychologically, it reflects how nurturing positive habits and virtues fosters resilience, emotional stability, and long-term personal growth. Another striking metaphor is found in the verse describing "life as transient vegetation" (Al-Hadid, 57:20). Here, worldly life is compared to plants that thrive after rain but soon wither and decay. This serves as a powerful reminder of the fleeting nature of material pursuits. From a psychological viewpoint, it encourages a shift in focus from temporary pleasures to enduring values like purpose, sincerity, and spiritual contentment – foundations of lasting mental well-being. The metaphor of "Allāh as Light" (An-Nur, 24:35) likens divine guidance to light that illuminates and guides the heart. This resonates with the innate human desire for clarity, meaning, and peace. Psychologically, it parallels the inner journey towards self-awareness, as divine light reveals inner truths, offering emotional clarity, tranquillity, and a rooted sense of identity.

The metaphor of "sealed hearts" (Al-Baqarah, 2:7) illustrates the consequences of persistently rejecting divine truth. It describes individuals who have shut themselves off from spiritual insight, resulting in emotional and spiritual numbness. From a psychological perspective, this parallels cognitive rigidity, where continual denial or avoidance of reality prevents growth, adaptability, and openness to new perspectives, often leading to internal conflict and psychological stagnation. Likewise, the verse that speaks of a "disease in the heart" (Al-Baqarah, 2:10) refers to spiritual afflictions such as doubt, hypocrisy, and inner unrest. This metaphor highlights how moral inconsistencies and dishonesty can deepen emotional suffering. Psychologically, it aligns with the concept of cognitive dissonance, when an individual holds contradictory beliefs or behaves in ways that conflict with their values, resulting in inner tension, weakened moral clarity, and emotional imbalance. The metaphor of "hardened hearts" (Al-Baqarah, 2:74) compares certain hearts to stone, resistant to change and to truth. Unlike rocks from which water may still flow, these hearts show no signs of responsiveness. This imagery reflects emotional desensitisation: when truth and guidance are consistently ignored, the heart loses its capacity for empathy, self-reflection, and change, thereby obstructing emotional healing and spiritual growth.

The verse on spiritual nourishment through rain (Al-An'am, 6:99) uses the image of rainfall bringing forth vegetation to symbolise divine guidance reviving the soul. Just as rain is essential for the earth to flourish, spiritual insight is vital for emotional and psychological renewal. This metaphor emphasises the importance of regularly engaging with revelation and reflection, which cultivate spiritual awareness and nourish a balanced, grounded psyche. Finally, metaphors such as "forgetting Allāh and forgetting oneself" (Al-Hashr, 59:19) and the "spider's web" (Al-'Ankabut, 29:41) explore the consequences of misplaced reliance and spiritual neglect. When one disconnects from the remembrance of Allāh, they lose sight of their true identity and purpose, leading to confusion and self-alienation. Likewise, relying on weak foundation, like a spider's fragile web, symbolises psychological fragility and vulnerability. These metaphors encourage self-reliance and reliance on Allāh (*Tawakkul*) as a source of emotional strength and spiritual stability.

The verse describing spiritual nourishment through rain (Al-An'am, 6:99) presents a powerful metaphor: rainfall bringing vegetation to life represents divine guidance rejuvenating the soul. Just as rain is essential for the earth to thrive, spiritual insight is important for emotional renewal and psychological well-being. This imagery highlights the need for consistent engagement with revelation and introspection to foster inner growth, spiritual clarity, and a grounded sense of self. Similarly, metaphors such as "forgetting Allāh and forgetting oneself" (Al-Hashr, 59:19) and the "spider's web" (Al-'Ankabut, 29:41) illustrate the dangers of spiritual neglect and misplaced dependence. When individuals lose connection with the remembrance of Allāh, they become estranged from their true identity and purpose, resulting in confusion and inner disorientation. The spider's web, symbolising weak reliance, reflects psychological fragility, placing trust in unstable foundations leads to emotional vulnerability and insecurity. These metaphors serve as reminders of the importance of both self-awareness and trust in Allāh, offering pathways to emotional resilience and spiritual strength. A summary of the metaphors, Qur'ān verses, explanations, and psychological insights is presented in Table 7.1.

In IINT, the use of Qur'ānic metaphors is thoughtfully adapted to suit each client's specific needs, cultural background, and personal challenges. Therapists carefully select metaphors that align with the individual's lived experiences, ensuring that the therapeutic dialogue remains meaningful and impactful. While this personalised approach enhances relevance and resonance within therapy, the broader application of Qur'ānic metaphors extends beyond individual sessions. These metaphors offer accessible, vivid illustrations of deep spiritual and moral truths, effectively communicating complex

Table 7.1 Metaphors, Qur'ān verses, explanations, and psychological insights

Metaphor	Qur'ānic verse	Interpretation	Psychological insight
Good word as a good tree	"Have you not considered how Allāh presents an example, [making] a good word like a good tree, whose root is firmly fixed and its branches [high] in the sky?" (Ibrahim, 14:24).	This parable represents the believer's righteous deeds, including their good words and actions. The believer is likened to the fruitful date palm, consistently producing good deeds that rise continually, both day and night.[a]	This metaphor emphasises the psychological and spiritual importance of good deeds.
Life as transient vegetation	"Know that the life of this world is but amusement and diversion and adornment and boasting to one another and competition in increase of wealth and children – like the example of a rain whose [resulting] plant growth pleases the tillers; then it dries and you see it turned yellow; then it becomes [scattered] debris" (Al-Hadid, 57:20).	This metaphor likens worldly life to transient vegetation that flourishes after rain but eventually withers, illustrating the fleeting nature of worldly pleasures.	Psychologically, it serves as a reminder of the impermanence of material pursuits and the importance of focusing on enduring, meaningful goals for long-term fulfillment.
Allāh as Light	"Allāh is the Light of the heavens and the earth. His Light is like a niche in which there is a lamp…" (An-Nur, 24:35).	Allāh enlightens the hearts of the believers among the dwellers of the heavens and the earth. (The similitude of His light) the light of the believers.[b]	From a psychological standpoint, it reflects the human desire for clarity and meaning, highlighting how clear guidance can provide a sense of comfort, inner peace, and a stronger sense of direction in life.
Sealed hearts	"Allāh has set a seal upon their hearts and upon their hearing, and over their vision is a veil." (Al-Baqarah, 2:7).	This metaphor indicated that Allāh has sealed up their hearts and ears and a covering has fallen over their eyes, and they have incurred the severest punishment.[c]	Psychologically, it illustrates how repeated rejection of truth can lead to cognitive rigidity, making individuals less receptive to new information or perspectives.

(*Continued*)

Table 7.1 (Continued)

Metaphor	Qur'ānic verse	Interpretation	Psychological insight
Disease in hearts	"In their hearts is disease, so Allāh has increased their disease; and for them is a painful punishment because they [habitually] used to lie." (Al-Baqarah, 2:10)	Disease is a metaphor for doubt, hypocrisy, conflict and darkness. so Allāh increased their doubt, hypocrisy, conflict and darkness. And they will have a painful torment in the Hereafter.[b]	This highlights the psychological concept of cognitive dissonance, where internal conflicts and dishonesty can exacerbate mental distress and ethical deterioration.
Hardened hearts	"Then your hearts became hardened after that, being like stones or even harder..." (Al-Baqarah, 2:74)	This metaphor describes the disbelievers' hearts as being harder than stones, emphasising their resistance to divine guidance. Unlike certain rocks from which rivers flow or water emerges, their hearts remain indifferent and unrelenting.	Psychologically, this reflects how repeated exposure to truth without acceptance can lead to desensitisation, making individuals less receptive to positive change and growth.
Spiritual nourishment	"And it is He who sends down rain from the sky, and We produce thereby the growth of all things." (Al-An'am 6:99)	It is He Who sends down water (rain) from the sky, and with it We bring forth vegetation of all kinds.[d] Metaphorically, rain represents God's blessings and guidance	Psychologically it is about revitalising hearts and promoting spiritual growth.
Self-awareness	"And be not like those who forgot Allāh, so He made them forget themselves." (Al-Hashr 59:19)	Man's real position in the world is that he is slave of only One God. The person who, in not know this truth, does not in fact know himself.[c]	Being God-conscious (*Taqwa*) and remembrance of Allāh are essential to prevent spiritual neglect.
Spider's web	"The example of those who take allies other than Allāh is like that of a spider who builds a house, and indeed, the weakest of houses is the house of a spider." (Al-'Ankabut 29:41)	Relying on anything other than Allāh is compared to a spider's web, fragile and easily destroyed, emphasising the weakness of such dependencies.	The spider's web symbolises psychological fragility. It reflects the instability of relying on superficial or temporary supports instead of building emotional resilience with reliance on Allāh (*Tawakkul*)

[a] Ibn Kathir. Quran 14:24 Tafsir Ibn Kathir
[b] Ibn 'Abbās Tanwîr al-Miqbās min Tafsîr Ibn 'Abbās
[c] A'la Maududi. Tafseer Tafheem-ul-Quran Syed Abu-al-A'la Maududi
[d] Muhammad Taqiud-Din alHilali

ideas to a wide audience. For example, plant metaphors, such as those symbolising the growth of faith or the benefits of charity, translate abstract teachings into familiar, tangible imagery. This not only aids comprehension but also encourages thoughtful reflection across varied contexts, regardless of one's background or level of religiosity. Thus, while IINT customises metaphor use for therapeutic effectiveness, the universal appeal of Qur'ānic metaphors makes them powerful tools for broader spiritual and psychological engagement.

As an Islāmic psychotherapist, part of their role can also encompass *da'wah* (Arabic: دعوة), which refers to the practice of inviting others to gain a deeper understanding of Islām and, where appropriate, encouraging its embrace.

As an Islāmic psychotherapist in their role in *da'wah* (Arabic: دعوة), which refers to the Islāmic practice of inviting others to understand and embrace Islām. In the Qur'ân, Allāh say:

$$\text{إِلَّا ٱلَّذِينَ ءَامَنُوا۟ وَعَمِلُوا۟ ٱلصَّـٰلِحَـٰتِ وَتَوَاصَوْا۟ بِٱلْحَقِّ وَتَوَاصَوْا۟ بِٱلصَّبْرِ}$$

- *Except for those who have believed and done righteous deeds and advised each other to truth and advised each other to patience.* (Asr 103:3, interpretation of the meaning)

In his exegesis, Muhammad Taqiud-Din alHilali explained the above verse as follows: "Except those who believe (in Islāmic Monotheism) and do righteous good deeds, and recommend one another to the truth (i.e. order one another to perform all kinds of good deeds (*Al-Ma'ruf*) which Allāh has ordained, and abstain from all kinds of sins and evil deeds (*Al-Munkar*) which Allāh has forbidden), and recommend one another to patience (for the sufferings, harms, and injuries which one may encounter in Allāh 's Cause during preaching His religion of Islāmic Monotheism or Jihad. Abdullah bin 'Amr bin Al-'As (May Allāh be pleased with them) reported: The Prophet (ﷺ) said, "Convey from me even an *Ayah* [verse] of the Qur'ân" (Bukhârî (a)). *Da'wah* employs these metaphors universally to communicate the core messages of Islām effectively to all.

Hadīth's metaphor

The Qur'ân frequently utilises metaphors without offering direct explanations; however, their meanings are clarified and contextualised through the sayings (*hadīth*) and practices (*Sunnah*) of the Prophet Muhammad (ﷺ). These Prophetic traditions act as an interpretive lens, helping to unpack the metaphorical language of the Qur'ân and illustrating how such metaphors can be applied in everyday life. By engaging with the *hadīth* and *Sunnah*, individuals can better understand the deeper significance of Qur'ānic metaphors, effectively connecting abstract ideas to real-world experiences. Research has also explored the cultural and social settings in which these metaphors appear within *hadīth* literature (Almutairi et al., 2024; Fouda, 2024), shedding light on the values and perspectives of the broader Islāmic community. Moreover, Fouda's (2024) study highlights the enduring relevance of these metaphors in offering moral guidance, shaping beliefs and behaviours, and reinforcing ethical and spiritual principles for contemporary Muslim life.

The *hadīth* literature of Prophet Muhammad (ﷺ) is rich in metaphorical language that conveys deep psychological and spiritual insights. One notable example is the metaphor of the mirror, which highlights the role of interpersonal relationships in self-awareness and personal development. When the Prophet (ﷺ) stated that "a believer is the mirror of his brother," it suggests that companions reflect one another's character and behaviour. This encourages a therapeutic approach rooted in compassionate feedback and the positive influence of supportive relationships. Another powerful metaphor found in the *hadīth* is the depiction of the Muslim community as a single body. Just as pain in one part of the body affects the whole, the suffering of one member of the *Ummah* should resonate with the entire community. This image promotes empathy, shared emotional responsibility, and collective healing, core principles in Islāmic psychology and a vital aspect of psychospiritual care. The metaphor of life as a transient journey, symbolised by a traveller resting briefly under the shade of a tree, encourages detachment from worldly distractions and reminds believers of the temporary nature of this life. Psychospiritually, this metaphor fosters resilience, reinforces spiritual purpose, and helps individuals endure hardships with a greater sense of meaning. It gently guides the believer towards preparing for the hereafter, where lasting peace and fulfilment await.

When addressing the concept of inner purification, the metaphor of sins falling like leaves offers a profound image of spiritual cleansing. According to prophetic teachings, engaging in *dhikr* (the remembrance of Allāh) through phrases such as *"Al-hamdulillāh"* (All praise is due to Allāh), *"Subḥān Allāh"* (Glory be to Allāh), *"Lā ilāha illallāh"* (There is no deity but Allāh), and *"Allāhu Akbar"* (Allāh is the Greatest), leads to sins being shed from the believer like leaves falling from a tree. This metaphor highlights *dhikr* as a form of spiritual detoxification, much like a tree renews itself by shedding its leaves. Psychologically, it provides a therapeutic pathway for releasing guilt and fostering moral renewal through consistent, reflective practice. Additionally, metaphors involving the senses and speech, such as the tongue as a sword or the eyes as windows to the soul, emphasise the importance of mindful use of one's faculties. By cultivating awareness of how each action and expression affects the soul, these metaphors nurture self-regulation, spiritual accountability, and a heightened moral consciousness, key components of holistic psychospiritual well-being.

Table 7.2 presents the metaphors, explanations, corresponding *hadīths*, and psychospiritual insights.

Table 7.2 Metaphors, explanations, corresponding *hadīths*, and psychospiritual insights

Metaphor	Hadith reference	Explanation	Psychospiritual insight
Mirror	A believer is the mirror of his brother. When he sees a fault in it, he should correct it. (Bukhārī (b))	Emphasises that the mirror reflects the true self – the beauty and weakness of the believer. The believer helps his friend by concealing his friend's fault from others and rectifying them.	This suggest that friends mirror each other's qualities highlights the profound impact of social connections on personal growth. Engaging with individuals who embody positive traits can inspire and reinforce similar behaviours within oneself.
Muslims as a single body	The similitude of believers in regard to mutual love, affection, fellow-feeling is that of one body; when any limb of it aches, the whole body aches, because of sleeplessness and fever (Muslim (a)).	Compares the Muslim community to a single body; when one part feels pain, the entire body shares in the suffering.	Emphasises empathy, solidarity, and collective responsibility within the *Ummah*, fostering a sense of unity and mutual support.
This World and the Hereafter	"Be in this world as if you were a stranger or a traveller." (Bukhārī (c))	Compares this world to the shade of a tree under which a traveler rests briefly during a long journey, highlighting its temporary nature.	Encourages detachment from materialism, reminding individuals of the transient nature of worldly life and the importance of focusing on the eternal hereafter.
Believer's sins as falling leaves	"Indeed, 'all praise is due to Allāh (*Al-Ḥamdulillāh*)' 'glory to Allāh (*Subḥān Allāh*)' 'none has the right to be worshipped by Allāh (*Lā ilāha Illallāh*)' and 'Allāh is the greatest (*Allāhu Akbar*)' cause the sins to fall from the worshipper, just as the leaves of this tree fall." (Tirmidhī).	A believer's sins are likened to leaves falling from a tree when repentance and good deeds are practiced.	Spiritual purification through the repetition of certain phrases. eaves falling from a tree symbolise the shedding of impurities. Just as trees naturally shed leaves to rejuvenate, engaging in the remembrance of Allāh (*dhikr*) helps cleanse the soul, removing spiritual burdens and renewing one's inner state.
Tongue as a Sword	Whoever believes in Allāh and the Last Day should speak what is good or keep silent. (Bukhārī (d)).	Warns about the potential harm of speech and the importance of speaking good or remaining silent.	The power of speech can build or destroy. Words can heal, inspire, or harm, so being mindful of speech and using it for positive purposes fosters peace, wisdom, and restraint, which aligns with psychological well-being.
Eyes as windows to the soul	The adultery of the eye is the lustful look and the adultery of the ears is listening to voluptuous (song or talk) and the adultery of the tongue is licentious speech and the adultery of the hand is the lustful grip (embrace) and the adultery of the feet is to walk (to the place) where he intends to commit adultery and the heart yearns and desires which he may or may not put into effect. (Muslim (b))	Suggests that one's gaze, ears, tongue touch, and action reflect inner thoughts and emotions, highlighting the need for purity in vision and intention.	This is a guide for ethical living, emphasising the interconnectedness of actions and inner states. It encourages individuals to be mindful of their sensory engagements and thoughts, promoting a balanced and spiritually conscious life.

The Metaphor-Islāmic Model

The Metaphor-Islāmic Model is a structured six-stage framework designed to integrate client-generated metaphors within the context of Islāmic psychotherapy, particularly in approaches like Islāmic Modified Narrative Therapy. The Metaphor-Islāmic Model utilises metaphors as instruments for exploration and healing, integrating therapeutic practices with Islāmic principles to enhance client engagement (Ahammed, 2010). Integrating Islāmic principles into therapeutic practices involves a structured six-step approach that aligns with spiritual and psychological growth. The stages include Listening (attending to content and intent); Identification of metaphor (*Istinbāṭ Al-Tamthīl*); Clarification and collaborative exploration *(Bayān wa Tafsīr)*; Validity through an Islāmic lens *(Tathabbut wa Tasdīq)*; Application and meaning-making (*Tadwīn wa Taṭbīq*); and Transformation and *tawakkul* (trust and renewal). Table 7.3 and Figure 7.1 present the Metaphor-Islāmic Model.

Table 7.3 Metaphor-Islāmic: A Six-Stage Model

Stage	Title	Description	Islāmic integration
1	Listening (Attending to content and intent)	Deep, respectful listening to both the contents and the niyyah (intent) behind them. The therapist is present with adab and empathy.	Anchored in "Who listen to speech and follow the best of it. Those are the ones Allāh has guided, and those are people of understanding." (Az Zumar 39:18).
2	Identification of metaphor (*Istinbāṭ Al-Tamthīl*)	Recognising the symbolic and metaphorical language used by the client, consciously or unconsciously.	Reflects the Qur'ânic or hadīth use of parables (amthāl) and symbolic imagery. Therapist identifies these in the client's narrative.
3	Clarification and collaborative exploration *(Bayān wa Tafsīr)*	Exploring the metaphor's meaning with the client, eliciting personal, emotional, and spiritual associations.	Parallels tafsīr methodology, unpacking layered meanings together. Encourages client agency and reflection.
4	Validity through an Islāmic lens *(Tathabbut wa Tasdīq)*	Evaluating whether the metaphor is valid or distorted based on Islāmic ethics, Qur'ânic or *hadīth*.	Involves referencing Prophetic wisdom or Islāmic metaphors to affirm or gently realign the metaphor's message.
5	Application and meaning-making (*Tadwīn wa Taṭbīq*)	Applying insights from the metaphor to life decisions, coping strategies, and moral behavior.	Supports transformation (*tazkiyah*) through metaphor, turning insight into action, anchored in Islāmic values.
6	Transformation and *Tawakkul* (Trust and renewal)	Emphasises renewed hope, trust in Allāh, and moving forward with purpose and divine reliance.	Draws on *tawakkul, sabr,* and *tajdīd al-niyyah* (renewal of intention) to inspire a forward-facing journey.

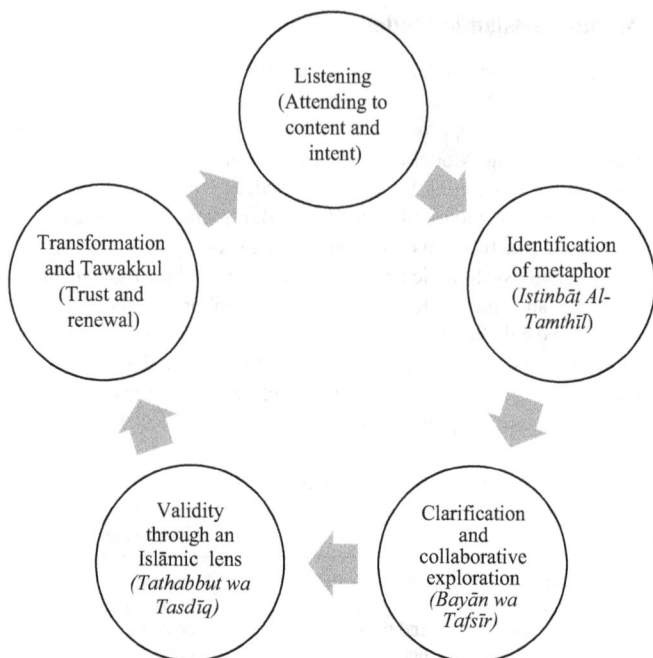

Figure 7.1 Metaphor-Islāmic Model.

The stages of identifying and interpreting metaphors involve a multi-step process rooted in attentive listening, thoughtful exploration, and application. First, one begins by fully understanding the speaker's content and intent before moving on to identify metaphors (*Istinbāṭ Al-Tamthīl*) embedded in the communication. Following this, metaphors are clarified and collaboratively explored (*Bayān wa Tafsīr*) to reveal deeper meanings. To ensure these metaphors align with Islāmic principles, their validity is carefully examined (*Tathabbut wa Tasdīq*). Finally, the insights gained are documented and applied (*Tadwīn wa Taṭbīq*) to create meaningful outcomes. Each stage emphasises the importance of thorough understanding, contextual relevance, and practical application, especially when viewed through an Islāmic lens.

Conclusion

Metaphor functions not simply as a linguistic tool but as a fundamental way in which individuals interpret and structure their experiences (Lakoff & Johnson, 2008). In therapeutic settings, metaphors offer a powerful and accessible method for clients to externalise internal struggles, articulate complex emotions, and reframe their understanding of personal challenges. Whether originating from the client or introduced by the therapist, metaphors facilitate narrative transformation, emotional insight, and greater cognitive flexibility (Angus & McLeod, 2004). In the realm of Islāmic psychotherapy, particularly within the developing approach of IINT, metaphor assumes an even more profound, spiritually grounded role. This framework draws deeply from the rich metaphorical language of the Qur'ān and *hadīth*, embedding psychological healing within a theocentric and spiritually resonant worldview. Qur'ānic metaphors, beyond their poetic beauty, function as spiritual diagnostics, offering insights that align closely with the lived realities and belief systems of Muslim clients. Similarly, the metaphors found in *hadīth* literature provide psychologically meaningful guidance, rooted in the prophetic model. From this foundation emerges the Metaphor-Islāmic Model, a culturally attuned and spiritually congruent therapeutic approach that integrates sacred metaphors with the core principles of narrative therapy, supporting holistic healing through both faith and psychology.

References

Ahammed, S. (2010). Applying Qur'ānic metaphors in counseling. *International Journal of Advanced Counselling, 32*, 248–255. https://doi.org/10.1007/s10447-010-9104-2.

Almutairi, M., Benneghrouzi, F. Z., & Zitouni, M. (2014). The workings and translatability of metaphors in eleven "Hadīth" *ONOMÁZEIN-Journal* of *Linguistics, Philology and Translation, 65* (September 2024), 01–18.

Angus, L. E., & Greenberg, L. S. (2011). Working with narrative in emotion-focused therapy: Changing stories, healing lives. *American Psychological Association.* https://doi.org/10.1037/12325-000.

Angus, L. E., & McLeod, J. (Eds.). (2004). *The handbook of narrative and psychotherapy: Practice, theory, and research.* Sage Publications, Inc. https://doi.org/10.4135/9781412973496.

Angus, L. E., & Rennie, D. L. (1988). Therapist participation in metaphor generation: Collaborative and noncollaborative styles. *Psychotherapy: Theory, Research, Practice, Training, 25*(4), 552–560. https://doi.org/10.1037/h0085381.

Armstrong, A. M., & Munro, l. (2018). Insider/outsider: A Muslim woman's adventure practicing 'alongside' narrative therapy. *Australian and New Zealand Journal of Family Therapy, 39*(2), 174–185.

Bukhârî (a). *Riyad as-Salihin 1380.* In-book reference: Book 12, Hadīth 5. https://sunnah.com/riyadussalihin:1380.

Bukhârî (b). *Al-Adab Al-Mufrad 238.* In-book reference: Book 12, Hadīth 1. English translation: Book 12, Hadīth 238. Hasan (Al-Albani). https://sunnah.com/adab:238.

Bukhârî (c). *Sahih al-Bukhârî 6416.* In-book reference: Book 81, Hadīth 5. USC-MSA web (English) reference: Vol. 8, Book 76, Hadīth 425. https://sunnah.com/bukhari:6416.

Bukhârî (d). *Sahih al-Bukhârî 6136.* In-book reference: Book 78, Hadīth 163. USC-MSA web (English) reference: Vol. 8, Book 73, Hadīth 158. https://sunnah.com/bukhari/78/163.

Fainsilber, L., & Ortony, A. (1987). Metaphorical uses of language in the expression of emotions. *Metaphor and Symbolic Activity*, 2, 239–250.

Fouda, M. M. I. M. (2024). Analysis of Conceptual Metaphor in the Prophetic Hadīth. 7(49), 546–527 ,(السوي قناة جامعة الإنسانية العلوم و الأداب كلية مجلة. https://doi.org/10.21608/jfhsc.2024.409284.

Killick, S., Curry, V., & Myles, P. (2016). The mighty metaphor: A collection of therapists' favourite metaphors and analogies. *The Cognitive Behaviour Therapist*, 9, e37. https://doi.org/10.1017/S1754470X16000210.

Kopp, R. R. (1995). *Metaphor therapy: Using client-generated metaphors in psychotherapy*. Brunner/Mazel.

Lakoff, G., & Johnson, M. (2008). *Metaphors we live by* (2nd ed.). University of Chicago Press.

Lloyd, J. (2017). Therapeutic use of metaphor: Cultural connectivity. *Journal of Experiential Psychotherapy*, 20(2), 3–10.

Lyddon, W. J., Clay, A. L., & Sparks, C. L. (2001). Metaphor and change in counseling. *Journal of Counseling & Development*, 79(3), 269–274.

Malkomsen, A., Røssberg, J. I., Dammen, T., Wilberg, T., Løvgren, A., Ulberg, R., & Evensen, J. (2022). How therapists in cognitive behavioral and psychodynamic therapy reflect upon the use of metaphors in therapy: A qualitative study. *BMC Psychiatry*, 22(1), 433. https://doi.org/10.1186/s12888-022-04083-y.

Martin, J., Cummings, A., & Halberg, E. (1992). Therapists' intentional use of metaphor: Memorability, clinical impact, and possible epistemic/motivational functions. *Journal of Consulting and Clinical Psychology*, 60, 143–145.

Mathieson, F., Jordan, J., Carter, J. D., & Stubbe, M. (2015). The metaphoric dance: Co-construction of metaphor in cognitive behaviour therapy. *The Cognitive Behaviour Therapist*, 8, e24. https://doi.org/10.1017/S1754470X15000628.

Sue, D. W., Sue, D., Neville, H. A., & Smith, L. (2022). *Counseling the culturally diverse: Theory and practice*. John Wiley & Sons.

Suhadi, J. (2011). Metaphor as a stylistic device of Islāmic teaching. MIQOT: *Jurnal Ilmu-ilmu KeIslāman, XXXV*(1), 187–202.

Tirmidhî. *Jami 'at- Tirmidhî 3533*. In-book reference : Book 48, Hadīth 164. English translation: Vol. 6, Book 45, Hadīth 3533. Hasan (Darussalam). https://sunnah.com/tirmidhi:3533.

Törneke, N. (2017). *Metaphor in practice: A professional's guide to using the science of language in psychotherapy*. Context Press/New Harbinger Publications.

Wagener, A. E. (2017). Metaphor in professional counseling. *The Professional Counsellor, 7*(2). https://tpcjournal.nbcc.org/metaphor-in-professional-counseling/

Wickman, S. A., Daniels, M. H., White, L. J. & Fesmire, S. A. (1999). A "primer" in conceptual metaphor for counsellors. *Journal of Counselling & Development*, 77, 389–394.

Witztum, E., van der Hart, O., & Friedman, B. (1988). The use of metaphors in psychotherapy. *Journal of Contemporary Psychotherapy*, 18(4), 270–290.

www.merriam-webster.com. Metaphor: Definition & Meaning – Merriam-Webster. https://www.merriam-webster.com.

Section 2

Clinical applications

8 Clinical applications of Islāmic Integrated Narrative Therapy

Introduction

Islāmic Integrated Narrative Therapy (IINT) offers a spiritually grounded approach to psychotherapy, designed specifically for Muslim clients. It is rooted in the Qur'ān, the Sunnah of the Prophet Muhammad (ﷺ), and broader Islāmic tradition. Rather than viewing clients solely through a psychological lens, IINT sees them as spiritual beings on a journey of *tawbah* (repentance), *islāh al-nafs* (self-reformation), and reconnection with Allāh. The therapist acts as a *rafīq* (companion), supporting clients through their struggles while integrating Islāmic values. This framework encourages clients to understand their hardships within the larger divine narrative of purpose, mercy, and redemption. A distinctive feature of IINT is its use of spiritual practices as central therapeutic tool, not just adjuncts. These include *dhikr* (remembrance), *du'ā'h* (supplication), *salāh* (prayer), *sadaqah* (charity), and *ruqyah* (spiritual healing).

Stories from the lives of the Prophets (عليهم السلام), along with personal accounts from the life of the Prophet Muhammad (ﷺ), serve as profound narrative tools that reflect clients' experiences of struggle, repentance, resilience, and the mercy of Allāh. For instance, the story of Prophet Yūnus (as) calling out to Allāh from the belly of the whale (Al-Anbiya 21:87) can symbolise a client's experience of despair and eventual relief. Similarly, the *hadīth* comparing the believer to a strong palm tree. Narrated Anas bin Malik (May Allāh be pleased with him) the Messenger of Allāh said

> "The parable of a goodly word is that of a goodly tree, whose root is firmly fixed, and its branches (reach) to the sky (Ibraheem 14:24 & 25)." And he said: "It is the date-palm." And the parable of an evil tree uprooted from the surface of the earth, having no stability (Ibraheem 14:26). He said: "It is the colocynth tree."
>
> (Tirmidhî (a))

This chapter explores these clinical strategies in depth, presenting practical examples and illustrating how client-generated metaphors can be woven

DOI: 10.4324/9781003584995-10

together with Qur'ānic and Prophetic metaphors to reconstruct narratives of brokenness into spiritually empowered stories of healing and renewal.

Therapeutic assessment: client's spirituality

In IINT, therapeutic sensitivity is a requisite, particularly when engaging with a client's spirituality and religious worldview. While standard narrative therapy assessments explore a client's social, emotional, and psychological experiences, an Islāmic framework broadens this to include the physical, social, psychological, and spiritual aspects of the client's life. Although assessment must still adhere to the ethical standards of the therapeutic setting or agency, this model introduces an added layer of responsibility – approaching the client's faith, beliefs, and spiritual struggles with deep cultural and religious sensitivity. This involves not only listening to how clients describe their suffering but also understanding how they interpret their experiences through an Islāmic perspective, including key concepts like *tawakkul* (reliance on God), *qadar* (divine decree), and *sabr* (patience). Building a strong therapeutic alliance in this context requires trust, respect for sacred meanings, and spiritual empathy. Such an approach enables clients to re-author their narratives in a way that is consistent with their Islāmic values, helping to restore their sense of purpose, dignity, and connection to Allāh.

In IINT, therapeutic sensitivity is essential when exploring a client's spirituality or relationship with faith, and this must be done with care, humility, and without judgement. Rather than beginning with direct or potentially intrusive questions like, "Do you pray five times a day?" or "How is your relationship with Allāh?" which may feel judgemental or moralising, the therapist adopts a compassionate, client-centred approach grounded in *adab* (Islāmic etiquette), humility, and deep respect for the client's unique spiritual journey. The goal is not to evaluate levels of religious observance, but to understand how the client connects with their faith, how it shapes their values, provides support, or presents challenges.

Sensitive and reflective questioning, aligned with both Islāmic *adab* and narrative therapy principles, allows for meaningful exploration without imposing moral expectations. These questions are crafted to gently invite reflection on the client's spiritual practices, such as *ṣalāh* (prayer), *dhikr* (remembrance of Allāh), or Qur'ān recitation, by focusing on how these practices affect their emotional and spiritual well-being. Rather than probing frequency or correctness, the therapist might ask how these practices bring comfort, grounding, or resilience during difficult times. This approach opens a respectful and safe space for the client to share their lived spiritual experiences. Another category of questions explores the client's evolving relationship with Islām and how faith integrates into their identity and life purpose. The aim is not to assess religious knowledge or outward practice, but to understand the personal significance of faith within the client's life story. Overall, the therapist engages

Table 8.1 Indirect questions exploring religiosity in Muslim clients

Thematic focus	Sample question	Purpose & non-intrusive
Personal faith practices	"Are there any spiritual practices that are important to you right now?"	Invites client to share current practices without evaluating frequency or correctness.
	"Do you find comfort in prayer or any other form of worship during stressful times?"	Explores emotional-spiritual coping without assuming religiosity.
	"What role does the Qur'ān or *dhikr* play in your life?"	Allows insight into faith integration without directly assessing observance.
	"Is there a particular routine or spiritual habit that helps ground you when you're feeling unsettled?"	Elicits spiritual resources with an emotional focus, not religious performance.
Faith identity and meaning	"How would you describe your connection with your faith these days?"	Encourages self-reflection on current spiritual experience, open to any answer.
	"Has your relationship with Islām changed over the years?"	Allows discussion of spiritual development or fluctuations over time without judgement.
	"What does being Muslim mean to you personally?"	Focuses on identity and meaning-making, not religious behaviour.
	"Do you feel that your faith gives you a sense of identity or purpose?"	Indirectly gauges spiritual centrality in life without moral expectation.

with the client's spirituality with compassion and reverence, recognising it as a deeply personal aspect of their healing and growth. Table 8.1 shows some indirect questions exploring religiosity in Muslim clients.

Therapeutic techniques and applications

In IINT, core techniques are thoughtfully designed to integrate Islāmic principles with narrative therapy practices, ensuring alignment with the client's religious and cultural values. While rooted in conventional narrative approaches, these techniques are adapted to reflect Islāmic teachings, rituals, and beliefs, making them both spiritually resonant and clinically effective. Therapists using IINT draw on a range of interventions that are flexible and responsive to each client's unique needs, presenting concerns, and life context. The goal is to promote healing and growth through a holistic process that nurtures both psychological well-being and spiritual connection. This dual focus enables deeper therapeutic engagement, where emotional challenges are addressed alongside spiritual development. Central to IINT are spiritual practices such as *dhikr* (remembrance of Allāh), *du'ā'h* (supplication), and *ṣalāh* (ritual prayer), which are not treated as supplementary tools but as integral components of the therapeutic journey. These practices offer clients meaningful ways to reconnect with Allāh, draw strength from their faith, and find comfort during times of distress. In addition, therapists may incorporate *Qur'ānic* narratives, Prophetic stories, and Islāmic metaphors into the therapeutic dialogue. These elements help clients reframe their struggles within the larger context of divine wisdom, encouraging reflection, resilience, and a renewed sense of purpose.

The choice of specific techniques is guided by careful assessment and ongoing collaboration with the client, ensuring that each intervention is tailored to their individual needs, values, and goals. Through this integrative approach, IINT supports clients in constructing spiritually meaningful and psychologically empowering life narratives.

Client's narrative (life story)

In IINT, exploring the client's narrative involves therapeutic questioning that honours both their personal experiences and their religious worldview. The aim is to uncover the significant events, meaningful moments, and life experiences that have shaped the client's identity and contributed to their current struggles or challenges. This narrative exploration offers clients a space to reflect on their past, recognise recurring patterns, and understand the personal meaning they assign to life events. The process centres on helping clients articulate their life story in a way that fosters self-awareness and empowerment. Open-ended, reflective questions are used to guide this exploration, allowing clients to express their journey in their own words. These questions highlight emotional turning points, influential relationships, and defining experiences, all while helping clients explore how these moments have influenced their sense of self. By reflecting on who they are, what they have experienced, and how they interpret these events through an Islāmic lens, clients are encouraged to reconstruct their narratives in a way that aligns with their values, faith, and personal growth. Table 8.2 shows the guiding questions in exploring the client's narrative.

In IINT, the process of externalising problems closely mirrors the traditional narrative therapy technique of separating the person from the problem. However, IINT deepens this approach by incorporating Islāmic spiritual principles that reframe struggles within a divine context. Instead of viewing emotional or psychological challenges as internal flaws, clients are supported in seeing these issues as tests (*ibtilā'*), opportunities for purification, or steps towards personal and spiritual growth, rooted in the concept of *qadar* (divine will). IINT emphasises *tawakkul* (reliance on Allāh) and invites clients to understand their struggles through a spiritual lens. Difficulties such as anger, anxiety, or low self-worth are not seen as intrinsic parts of one's identity, but

Table 8.2 Guiding questions in exploring the client's narrative

Case vignette	*Guiding questions*
Zayd, a 29-year-old student, describes his academic failure as a "breaking point." He feels he has disappointed his family and has lost his sense of direction and self-worth. He used to see himself as a high achiever and feels ashamed of his recent performance.	• If you were to share this moment in your life with someone, how would you describe it? • Reflecting on your life up until now, how would you tell your story? • Which significant events or turning points do you think have had the most influence on who you are today? • Which parts of your life narrative do you believe have had the biggest impact on shaping who you are? • What moments stand out as the most defining in your journey so far? • Can you recall a time when you felt genuinely proud of something you accomplished? • Can you remember a time when you felt aligned with your purpose or on the right path? What made it meaningful? • How did your family or community shape your perspective on success and failure? • Which aspects of your past do you still feel connected to in your life today? • Are there any recurring themes or patterns in your life that you've noticed? • If you were to give a name to this phase of your journey, what would it be? • What role do you see yourself playing in your life story at this moment? • What specific experiences or moments have had the most influence on who you are today?"

as external challenges that one is facing, part of the human experience and the journey towards self-betterment and closeness to Allāh. For instance, rather than internalising negative beliefs like "I am a failure" or "I am an angry person," the client is guided to reframe these as, "I am facing the challenge of anger," or "I am struggling with feelings of failure." This shift reduces self-blame, preserves dignity, and encourages proactive engagement with the issue. It reinforces the belief that the self is inherently noble and capable of change, in line with Islāmic teachings about the *fitrah* (natural purity) of the human self. Table 8.3 presents a comparison of externalisation in narrative therapy and IINT.

In cases where a client expresses statements like "I am always anxious" or "I'm such an angry person," both narrative therapy and IINT work to separate the problem from the person's identity. The therapist does not affirm the idea that the client *is* the problem, but instead helps them recognise emotions like anger or anxiety as external challenges, issues they are experiencing, not characteristics that define them. In the Islāmic framework,

Table 8.3 Comparing externalisation of a problem

Client's Statement	Therapist's reframe (General perspective)	Therapist's reframe (Islāmic perspective).
"I am always anxious."	"Anxiety seems to be something you are dealing with, but it is not who you are. It is something you can face and manage."	"Anxiety is a test that Allāh has placed before you. Let us explore how you can manage this test while staying true to your values."
"I'm such an angry person."	"Anger seems to be something you are experiencing, but it is not who you are. It is something you can work through and manage."	"Anger is a test that Allāh has placed before you. Let us explore how you can manage this test while staying true to your values."

this process is further enriched by the understanding that such struggles are not just psychological issues, but also spiritual tests (*ibtilā'*) from Allāh. Rather than viewing themselves as inherently flawed, clients are supported in seeing these challenges as temporary difficulties that can be managed through faith, patience, and reliance on Allāh. This perspective reinforces the belief that each struggle is an opportunity for spiritual growth and drawing closer to Allāh. Externalisation allows clients to separate their struggles from their identity, while reframing offers a faith-based lens to view these challenges as divine tests, a means of purification, and opportunities for spiritual growth.

Therapeutic reframing through Qur'ânic verses

After a problem is externalised, the next step in therapy is reframing. That involves changing the meaning or interpretation of a problem, helping clients view their struggles as opportunities for growth rather than fixed limitations. Reframing can be initiated by either the therapist or the client. Therapist-led reframing draws on psychological knowledge, Islāmic teachings, and therapeutic insight to offer alternative interpretations. For example, a therapist might suggest that a client's sense of failure is not a personal flaw, but a temporary setback or a learning experience, encouraging hope and growth. Client-led reframing occurs when the client begins to reinterpret their experiences through reflection or emerging insight. For instance, they may come to view anxiety not as a personal weakness, but as a natural response they can learn to manage. This form of reframing is especially empowering, as it fosters autonomy and self-awareness. Whether guided by the therapist or emerging from the client, reframing transforms how situations are perceived, fostering resilience, self-compassion, and a faith-aligned sense of empowerment.

The therapist may use these Qur'ânic verses as reminders that struggles are part of a divine plan to develop resilience, patience, and reliance on Allāh. In the Qur'ân, Allāh mentions that trials are inevitable, but they are also part of a divine plan designed to purify and strengthen believers. Allāh says in the Qur'ân:

وَلَنَبْلُوَنَّكُم بِشَىْءٍ مِّنَ ٱلْخَوْفِ وَٱلْجُوعِ وَنَقْصٍ مِّنَ ٱلْأَمْوَلِ وَٱلْأَنفُسِ وَٱلثَّمَرَٰتِ ۗ وَبَشِّرِ ٱلصَّٰبِرِينَ

- *And we will certainly test you with something of fear, hunger, loss of wealth, lives, and fruits. But give good tidings to the patient (Sabr).* (Al-Baqarah 2:155, interpretation of the meaning)

These challenges are reframed as tests from Allāh, aligning with the Islāmic view that life's difficulties (*fitnah*) are part of a divine plan to purify and strengthen believers.

The therapist can offer a perspective that challenges the perception of overwhelming or unmanageable struggles. When individuals face difficulties, they may feel burdened or incapable of handling them. The following verses of the Qur'ân highlight may be used in the reframing process when client presents a perspective that struggles are overwhelming or beyond one's ability to handle.

لَا يُكَلِّفُ ٱللَّهُ نَفْسًا إِلَّا وُسْعَهَا ۚ

- *Allāh does not charge a soul except [with that within] its capacity* (Al-Baqarah 2:286, interpretation of the meaning).

This verse aligns with reframing by offering a perspective that challenges the perception of overwhelming or unmanageable struggles. When individuals face difficulties, they may feel burdened or incapable of handling them. Reframing this belief, guided by the verse, helps clients see their challenges as something they are equipped to handle, given their inherent strength and the support of Allāh. It emphasises that their struggles are not beyond their capacity, but rather opportunities for growth, which can empower the individual to face and manage their challenges with a sense of resilience and self-efficacy.

وَٱلَّذِينَ جَٰهَدُوا۟ فِينَا لَنَهْدِيَنَّهُمْ سُبُلَنَا ۚ وَإِنَّ ٱللَّهَ لَمَعَ ٱلْمُحْسِنِينَ

- *And those who strive for Us – We will surely guide them to Our ways. And indeed, Allāh is with the doers of good.* (Al-Ankabut 29:69, interpretation of the meaning)

According to the exegesis of Syed Abul A'la Maududi, the verse reassures that Allāh does not abandon those who sincerely strive in His cause, even against overwhelming odds; rather, He guides, supports, and opens paths towards Him. He provides direction, discernment, and light at every stage, enabling them to seek His approval. This verse powerfully reframes effort and struggle, not as burdens, but as meaningful acts of *Jihād fī sabīlillāh* (striving in the path of Allāh) that foster spiritual and personal growth. It shifts the perspective from viewing hardships as punishments or misfortunes to recognising them as purposeful, divinely guided challenges. This interpretation reinforces key Islāmic values of resilience, perseverance, and trust in Allāh, encouraging believers to see their struggles as pathways to divine closeness and inner strength. In both therapist-led and client-led reframing, individuals are guided to view their difficulties from a new perspective, either as manageable challenges or as meaningful opportunities for personal and spiritual growth. This aligns with the core aim of therapeutic reframing: transforming the perception of struggles from burdens into catalysts for resilience, healing, and transformation.

The following is an example of a client-generated reframing. Fatima, a 35-year-old woman, struggles with the recent loss of her father, which has left her feeling emotionally overwhelmed and spiritually disconnected. During a session, the therapist gently asks, "Can you think of a moment when your faith offered you some comfort in this period of grief?" This invitation encourages Fatima to explore her inner resources. She pauses, then shares how a particular Qur'ānic verse helped her during her most difficult nights:

قَالُوٓا۟ إِنَّا لِلَّهِ وَإِنَّآ إِلَيْهِ رَٰجِعُونَ

- *Indeed, we belong to Allāh, and indeed to Him we will return.* (Al-Baqarah 2:156, interpretation of the meaning)

Reflecting on this, Fatima expresses that while the pain of loss is still present, the verse reminds her that death is a return to Allāh, and that her father is now in His care. She begins to reframe the loss not solely as a painful separation, but as part of a divine process that every soul must undergo. This shift in perception, prompted by her own faith and insight, allows her to hold her grief with greater compassion and a sense of spiritual meaning. In this way, the reframing is initiated by the client, and supported by the therapist through open-ended, faith-sensitive inquiry.

Exploring strength and resilience through faith

In IINT, the assessment process focuses not only on the client's strengths, skills, attitudes, and competencies but also includes a vital spiritual dimension. This approach explores how the client's faith and spiritual experiences have contributed to their resilience and ability to cope with adversity. By examining practices such as reliance on Allāh, prayer, and other Islāmic principles, the therapist helps the client reflect on how their beliefs have supported them through past challenges. Through guided conversation, the therapist works with the client to identify spiritual resources, recognise previously overlooked

Table 8.4 Types of questions to explore strengths through faith

Category	Questions
Reflecting on past strengths in difficult times	"Can you think of a time when you faced a major challenge or hardship? How did your faith help you through that experience?"
	"Tell me about a time when you felt particularly strong because of your connection to your faith. What did you do or think that helped you hold on?"
	"In past struggles, were there moments where you felt Allāh's guidance or mercy in a way that gave you hope or strength?"
Exploring the role of spiritual practices in coping	"When you faced difficulties in the past, were there specific prayers, supplications, or verses from the Qur'ān that brought you peace or clarity?"
	"How did your connection to prayer or *dhikr* affect your ability to cope with tough situations?"
	"Do you remember a time when turning to your faith helped you make an important decision during a difficult moment?"
Resilience through faith and values	"What values from Islām (e.g., *sabr* – patience, *tawakkul* – trust in Allāh, or *qadar* – acceptance of divine decree) have been especially important for you when facing life's challenges?"
	"Has there been a time when you felt like giving up, but your faith helped you stay resilient and continue moving forward?"
	"What do you think your faith has taught you about handling adversity, and how does that apply to your current situation?"
Identifying spiritual resources	"Can you recall any moments where you turned to Allah for help, and how did that shape your understanding of your strength?"
	"Are there any stories from the life of the Prophet Muhammad (ﷺ) or other figures in Islām that have inspired you to overcome challenges?"
	"Do you feel there are hidden spiritual resources within you that you haven't yet fully tapped into? What might they be?"

inner strengths rooted in faith, and deepen their awareness of how Islām has empowered them during difficult times. Table 8.4 provides a summary of the types of questions to explore strengths through faith. This table organises the questions by category and clearly shows how they can be used to explore the client's strengths, spiritual practices, and resilience through their faith in an IINT's context.

The following case vignette demonstrates how a therapist can gently guide a client to reflect on past challenges and uncover the ways in which their Islāmic faith, spiritual practices, and beliefs served as sources of strength, hope, and emotional resilience. Through thoughtful, non-intrusive questioning, the therapist helps the client reconnect with empowering spiritual

Table 8.5 Case Vignette: Therapist's exploration of strength and resilience through faith

Client background	A woman in her 30s, experiencing anxiety and hopelessness after losing her job during an economic downturn.
Initial therapist question	• "I understand that this loss has been tough on you. Could you share a moment from your past when you've gone through a similar struggle and what helped you get through that?"
Client's response	The client recalls a painful breakup from years ago. She felt emotionally disconnected but found peace and clarity through reading the Qur'ān and engaging in regular *dhikr*.
Follow-up questions	• "You mentioned the Qur'ān and *dhikr* helped you find peace. What was it about these practices that made you feel more grounded?" • "How did your faith help you shift from feeling lost to feeling more hopeful during that time?"

experiences and recognise internal resources they may have overlooked. Table 8.5 presents a case vignette based on the therapist's exploration of strength and resilience through faith.

As the client reflects on her experience, the therapist may gently notice and explore any specific Qur'ānic verses that held personal meaning or provided comfort during her struggle. Highlighting these connections can deepen the client's sense of spiritual grounding and foster a renewed awareness of her link to something greater than herself, namely, her relationship with Allāh. For instance, if the client mentions feeling a sense of calm or surrender in the face of uncertainty, the therapist might thoughtfully introduce Surah At-Tawbah (9:51):

قُل لَّن يُصِيبَنَآ إِلَّا مَا كَتَبَ ٱللَّهُ لَنَا هُوَ مَوْلَىٰنَا ۚ وَعَلَى ٱللَّهِ فَلْيَتَوَكَّلِ ٱلْمُؤْمِنُونَ

- *Say, "Never will we be struck except by what Allāh has decreed for us; He is our protector." And upon Allāh let the believers rely.* (At-Tawbah 9:51, interpretation of the meaning)

This verse can gently affirm the concept of *tawakkul*, offering the client a profound spiritual anchor. It reinforces her inner strength and faith-based resilience, reminding her that every challenge she faces is not random but part of a divinely ordained journey. It may help her embrace the belief that divine decree shapes her life with purpose, and that surrendering to Allāh's wisdom can bring peace, direction, and hope amidst uncertainty. The therapist might then say:

- "It seems that your faith in Allāh's wisdom and the concept of *tawakkul* (trust in Allāh) was something that carried you through both that difficult time and this present situation. How can you bring that same sense of trust and resilience into your current challenge?"

This line of questioning helps the client recognise that their spiritual practices are not just rituals but powerful sources of inner strength that they can draw upon in times of crisis.

Du'ā'h (supplication)

The following case vignette presents Ahmed, a 25-year-old university student experiencing severe anxiety primarily linked to academic demands and societal expectations. From a psycho-spiritual perspective, Ahmed's anxiety can be conceptualised as a product of both external stressors, such as performance pressures and the desire to meet communal standards, and internal conflicts related to self-worth and perceived competence. These dynamics contribute to persistent feelings of inadequacy and an intense fear of failure, further reinforced by a deep-seated need for validation and societal approval. Within the therapeutic setting, the practitioner gently invites Ahmed into reflective inquiry by asking, "Can you recall an instance when your faith supported you in navigating fear or uncertainty?"

Therapist: "*Ahmed, earlier you mentioned that presentations make you feel overwhelmed. I wonder-has there been a time when your faith helped you get through such moments of fear or uncertainty?*"
Ahmed: "*Yes, definitely. Before any big presentation or exam, I always recite a du'ā that Prophet Mūsā made when he had to speak to Pharaoh. It really calms me down.*"
Therapist: "*That's powerful. Could you share that du'āh with me?*"
Ahmed: "*Sure. It's from Surah Ṭāhā:*

قَالَ رَبِّ ٱشۡرَحۡ لِى صَدۡرِى
وَيَسِّرۡ لِىٓ أَمۡرِى
وَٱحۡلُلۡ عُقۡدَةً مِّن لِّسَانِى
يَفۡقَهُواْ قَوۡلِى

* *Rabbi ishrah lī ṣadrī, wa yassir lī amrī, waḥlul 'uqdatan min lisānī, yafqahū qawlī.' It means: "My Lord, expand [i.e. relax] for me my breast [with assurance]*
    And ease for me my task. And untie the knot from my tongue. That they may understand my speech. (Ṭāhā 20:25–28, interpretation of the meaning)

Therapist: "*That's beautiful. How do you feel when you recite it?*"
Ahmed: "*It makes me feel grounded, like I'm not alone. It reminds me that success isn't just about me, it's about trusting Allāh and doing my best.*"

Therapist:	*"That connection to Prophet Mūsā and his moment of vulnerability sounds deeply reassuring. Would you like to explore more ways we can integrate such spiritual resources into your daily coping strategies?"*
Ahmed:	*"Yes, I think that would really help."*

Ahmed's therapeutic journey illustrates the profound impact of connecting with the supplication of Prophet Mūsā (ʿalayhi as-salām) as a means of healing and transformation. By regularly reciting the Prophet's duʿāʾ from Sūrat Ṭāhā (20:25–28), Ahmed begins to see his own struggles reflected in a sacred narrative, drawing strength from the example of a Prophet who confronted fear through trust in divine support. This spiritual identification fosters a sense of solidarity and purpose, reframing anxious moments as opportunities for growth through faith.

The *duʿāʾh* serves not merely as a prayer, but as a symbolic anchor, reminding Ahmed that he is sustained by a source greater than himself. From a psycho-spiritual perspective, the practice of reciting this prayer functions as a structured and meaningful form of emotional regulation. The specific requests within the *duʿāʾh*, seeking clarity, ease, and the untying of internal knots, directly address Ahmed's performance-related anxiety, while reinforcing reliance on Allāh over self-reliance alone. The therapist's guidance in integrating this supplication into daily life, along with introducing other spiritual

Table 8.6 Outlining case vignette integrating supplication in therapy

Component	Details
Client	Ahmed, a 25-year-old student struggling with severe anxiety related to academic performance and societal expectations.
Therapeutic intervention	The therapist invites Ahmed to reflect on past spiritual experiences by asking, "Tell me about a time when your faith helped you overcome feelings of fear or uncertainty."
Spiritual practice	Ahmed recalls his habit of reciting the duʿā (supplication) for ease: "My Lord, expand [i.e. relax] for me my breast [with assurance]. And ease for me my task. And untie the knot from my tongue. That they may understand my speech. (Ṭāhā 20:25–28, interpretation of the meaning)
Client's reflection	Ahmed shares that this practice calms him before presentations and reminds him that success lies in trusting Allāh's wisdom, which helps him manage his anxiety.
Therapeutic outcome	Through the session, Ahmed gains confidence and integrates this spiritual practice into his coping strategies, feeling more at peace with his academic challenges.
Spiritual integration in therapy	The therapist encourages Ahmed to continue using this duʿā regularly, while also exploring other faith-based practices, such as reflecting on tawakkul (trust in Allāh), to further build resilience.

practices, empowers Ahmed to develop a faith-informed coping toolkit. Over time, the consistency of these practices not only alleviates his anxiety but also strengthens his spiritual resilience and confidence, fostering a more grounded and hopeful outlook. Table 8.6 outlines a case vignette integrating supplication in therapy.

Dhikr therapy (remembrance of Allāh)

Dhikr therapy, when integrated with the stages of narrative therapy, offers a spiritually grounded approach for clients to re-author their internal narratives, manage emotions, and reconnect with divine purpose. It can be practiced independently or under therapeutic guidance, ideally in solitude, allowing for deep reflection and spiritual connection. Importantly, *dhikr* must remain within the bounds of Islāmic teachings. However, it is important to emphasise that the application of *dhikr* must remain within the boundaries of Islāmic teachings. It is not permissible if it includes elements of *shirk* (associating partners with Allāh), such as the pre-Islāmic *Talbiyah*, or phrases that are theologically inappropriate, like saying "Peace be upon Allāh from His slaves," which was rejected in the early days of Islām. Such utterances misrepresent the proper etiquette and theology of addressing Allāh and must be strictly avoided in both personal and therapeutic contexts (Islāmqa, 2024). The Prophet (ﷺ) said: "Do not say 'Peace (*As-Salam*) be upon Allāh, for Allāh is *As-Salam*.'" Rather say:

> At-tahiyyatu lillahi was-salawatu wat-tayyibat, as-salamu ʿalaika ayyuhan-Nabiyyu wa rahmatAllāhi wa baraktuhu. As-salamu ʿalaina wa ʿala ʿibad illahis-salihin, ashahdu an la illaha ill-Allāh wa ashhadu anna Muhammadan ʿabduhu wa rasuluhu (Allāh compliments, prayers and pure words are due to Allāh. Peace be upon you, O Prophet, and the mercy of Allāh and his blessings. Peace be upon us and upon the righteous slaves of Allāh. I bear witness that none has the right to be worshipped except Allāh, and I bear witness that Muhammad is His slave and Messenger).
>
> (An-Nasa'i)

Dhikr includes reciting the Qur'ân, uttering phrases seeking forgiveness from Allāh, like (*Astaghfirullah*), Glory be to Allāh (*Subhan Allāh*), Praise be to Allāh (*Alhamdulillah*), there is no deity but Allāh (*La ilaha illa Allāh*), Allāh is the Greatest (*Allāhu Akbar*), there is no power or strength except with Allāh (*La hawlawala quwwata illa billah*) and invoking the names of Allāh.

The process begins with a sincere intention (*niyyah*) or example: *"I intend to remember Allāh to find peace and calm in my heart."* The client then selects a quiet, distraction-free environment conducive to reflection. This is followed by a deep breathing exercise: inhaling for 3–5 seconds, holding for 5 seconds, and exhaling slowly, which relaxes the body and focuses the mind. The practice formally starts by seeking protection through *"A`ūdhu billāhi min ash-shayṭān ir-rajīm"* and invoking *"Bismillāh ir-Raḥmān ir-Raḥīm,"* spiritually preparing the heart and mind for remembrance. The next step (optional) is for the therapist to begin by gently encouraging the client to contemplate the Qur'ânic verse:

ٱلَّذِينَ ءَامَنُواْ وَتَطۡمَئِنُّ قُلُوبُهُم بِذِكۡرِ ٱللَّهِ ۗ أَلَا بِذِكۡرِ ٱللَّهِ تَطۡمَئِنُّ ٱلۡقُلُوبُ

- *Those who have believed and whose hearts are assured by the remembrance of Allāh. Unquestionably, by the remembrance of Allāh hearts are assured.* (Ar-Ra`d 13:28, interpretation of the meaning)

This verse emphasises the deep peace and emotional stability that arise from the remembrance of Allāh (dhikr). The term "assured" conveys that *dhikr* offers more than just momentary comfort, it provides lasting inner tranquility and spiritual confidence. In clinical settings, this verse can be used to illustrate the therapeutic benefits of spiritual practices like *dhikr*, especially in promoting emotional regulation. For clients experiencing anxiety, agitation, or emotional distress, *dhikr* serves as a grounding tool that nurtures a sense of calm. In alignment with the verse, this connection to the Divine enables individuals to better cope with life's difficulties. For those dealing with trauma or post-traumatic stress, the verse can be used to highlight how *dhikr* fosters a sense of safety and spiritual reassurance. As indicated, remembrance of Allāh functions as a protective inner resource, offering comfort and steadiness during emotional turmoil. Basic dhikr involves reciting phrases such as *"Subḥān Allāh"* (Glory be to Allāh), *"Alḥamdulillāh"* (Praise be to Allāh), *"Allāhu Akbar"* (Allāh is the Greatest), and *"Lā ilāha illa Allāh"* (There is no deity but Allāh), with focused attention on their meanings. This contemplative recitation helps clients foster a deeper connection with Allāh. During this stage, contemplation is key; clients are encouraged to reflect on the words and remain present, with the therapist gently redirecting focus if needed.

To enhance spiritual depth, visualisation can be added. For instance, while reciting *"Subḥān Allāh,"* the client may visualise aspects of Allāh's creation, like the sky or ocean, strengthening their emotional and spiritual engagement. Sessions end with a *du`ā'h*, such as "Thank You, Allāh, for granting me the chance to remember You," promoting gratitude and closure. This structured yet simple process supports emotional regulation, relieves anxiety, and reinforces spiritual well-being. Table 8.7 outlines a step-by-step guide to implementing *Dhikr* therapy in clinical settings.

The *masbahah* (also known as *tasbih* or prayer beads) is a tool used to support *dhikr* and its use is generally considered permissible. While some scholars prefer counting *dhikr* on the fingers, citing the Prophet's (ﷺ) practice and the *hadīth* that fingers will testify on the Day of Judgement, using

Table 8.7 Outlining the procedure for a client to start *Dhikr* therapy

Step	Action	Details
Set the intention (*niyyah*)	Begin with the intention to engage in dhikr for peace and healing.	Example: "I intend to remember Allāh to find peace and calm in my heart."
Choose a comfortable setting	Find a quiet, peaceful space free from distractions.	Ensure the client is comfortable and spiritually focused.
Focus on breathing	Guide the client through deep breathing.	Inhale deeply for 3–5 seconds, hold for 5 seconds, and exhale slowly. Repeat 2–3 times.
Begin with *Bismillah*	Start with seeking refuge from shayṭān and invoking Allāh's name.	*"A'udhu billahi min ash-shayṭān ir-rajīm"* and *"Bismillāh ir-Raḥmān ir-Raḥīm."*
Contemplate the Qur'ānic verse:	Reflect on the Qur'ānic verse for spiritual grounding.	Those who have believed and whose hearts are assured by the remembrance of Allāh. Unquestionably, by the remembrance of Allāh hearts are assured. (Ar-Ra'd 13:28, interpretation of the meaning)
Recite basic *Dhikr* phrases	Introduce simple *dhikr* phrases.	Example: *"Subḥān Allāh"*, *"Alḥamdulillāh"*, *"Allāhu Akbar"*, *"Lā ilāha illa Allāh."*
Contemplate and be present	Encourage the client to engage in deep contemplation and while reciting the *dhikr*.	Gently bring the client's focus back to the *dhikr* if the mind wanders.
Visualisation (optional)	Use visualisation for deeper engagement.	Example: Visualise the beauty and vastness of Allāh's creation, such as the sky, oceans, mountains, and nature, while saying *"Subḥān Allāh"* (Glory be to Allāh).
End with a *Du'a'h* (supplication)	Close the session with a prayer for peace, healing, and strength.	Example: Thank You, Allāh, for granting me the chance to remember You."

the *masbahah* is not classified as *bid'ah* (innovation). Shaykh Ibn 'Uthaymīn explained that although fingers are better for *tasbih,* the *masbahah* has precedent among the companions who used pebbles, and it is not haram. However, he warned that using the *masbahah* might lead to distraction or showing off, especially when using elaborate beads. In therapy, clients may be encouraged to include regular *dhikr* in their daily routine to support emotional regulation. Therapists can invite reflection by asking how clients feel when they focus on Allāh during times of anxiety or stress. With consistency, this practice can help reframe distressing thoughts and foster a deeper sense of spiritual calm and security.

Ṣalāh (prayer)

In clinical practice, *ṣalāh* can be integrated as a spiritual intervention to support emotional regulation, stress reduction, and inner reflection. According to Tan (1996), this is known as explicit integration, where prayer becomes part of the therapeutic process. *Ṣalāh*, the prescribed ritual prayer in Islām, is not only a spiritual act but also offers therapeutic benefits. Its physical movements, such as bowing and prostration, promote grounding and relaxation, helping to calm the nervous system. Exploring a client's relationship with prayer can provide insight into their spiritual worldview, coping mechanisms, and emotional resilience. Understanding how a client engages with *ṣalāh* reveals personal sources of strength and meaning during hardship. By incorporating discussions about prayer, the therapist can guide clients to access these spiritual tools for healing and emotional stability. Reflecting on one's inner struggles through the lens of prayer fosters greater self-awareness and helps promote peace through spiritual connection.

Case example: Sarah and the integration of Salāh in therapy

Sarah, a 30-year-old manager in a high-pressure marketing firm, sought therapy for persistent anxiety and insomnia driven by chronic workplace stress. Despite trying common techniques like breathing exercises and meditation apps, she remained overwhelmed, physically tense, and mentally exhausted. Her therapist, noting the importance of faith in her life, introduced the idea of incorporating *ṣalāh* (Islāmic prayer) into her treatment. The therapist explained how the physical and contemplative aspects of *ṣalāh*, especially bowing and prostration, could help with emotional regulation and physical relaxation. Open to faith-based practices, Sarah began including *ṣalāh* in her daily routine. Though she initially struggled to focus, she soon noticed brief moments of calm during prayer, particularly in prostration, which helped relieve tension in her shoulders and neck. The therapist encouraged her to reflect by journaling after each prayer, which helped Sarah recognise emotional patterns and better understand her triggers. Over time, she reported improved sleep and reduced anxiety. The structured timing of *ṣalāh* introduced rhythm into her day, helping regulate her schedule and calm her mind before bed. Prayer also became a coping tool, during stressful work moments, she would pause for brief supplications to emotionally reset. Through consistent engagement with *ṣalāh*, Sarah felt more grounded and resilient, discovering a deeper sense of peace and emotional stability rooted in her spiritual practice.

Integrating prayer into Sarah's therapy allowed her to deepen her spiritual connection, which in turn supported emotional resilience and inner peace. As her relationship with *ṣalāh* grew, Sarah began reframing her stress through the lens of her faith, aligning the themes of her prayers, like seeking peace and relief from anxiety, with her therapeutic goals. This shift in perspective helped her manage stress more effectively, reinforcing the healing power of faith in her daily life. Her case underscores the value of incorporating spiritual practices into therapy for clients who identify with a religious framework. Professor Dr. Malik Badri, a pioneer in Islāmic psychology, shared an example of a therapist who integrated *wudu* (ablution) followed by two units of *rak'ah* (prayer) into sessions with Muslim clients. This approach supported spiritual and emotional cleansing while promoting

Table 8.8 Summarising the key aspects of Sarah's case

Aspect	Details	Outcome/benefit
Client's profile	Sarah, 30 years old, manager at a marketing firm, experiencing anxiety, insomnia, and stress.	N/A
Presenting issues	Anxiety, insomnia, work-related stress, physical tension in shoulders and neck, racing thoughts.	These issues led Sarah to seek therapy, affecting her work and personal life.
Spiritual practice introduced	Salāh (Islāmic prayer) as a tool for emotional regulation, spiritual reflection, and stress management.	Prayer was used to ground Sarah, promoting calm and helping her regulate emotional responses.
Therapeutic approach	Encouraged daily salāh, with a focus on the contents of the Qur'ânic recitation. Suggested journaling after prayer.	The combination of prayer, reflection, and physical movements in salāh helped Sarah engage in therapeutic progress.
Therapist's goals	Manage anxiety, improve sleep, relieve physical tension, promote emotional balance and spiritual connection.	The therapist integrated spiritual practices with conventional therapy, focusing on holistic well-being.
Sarah's engagement with prayer	Initially struggled with focus, gradually noticed calm moments during prayer, began journaling to reflect.	Increased engagement with prayer led to more clarity, calmness, and connection with her emotions.
Outcomes after several weeks	Reduction in anxiety, better sleep, reduced physical tension, greater emotional balance and grounding.	Sarah reported feeling "less anxious," more grounded, and experienced improved sleep and resilience.
Additional benefits noted	Prayer provided spiritual clarity, moments of reflection, and a tool to reset emotional states at work.	Prayer helped Sarah gain new perspectives, better manage work stress, and reframe negative thoughts.
Holistic impact	Integration of spiritual practice with Islāmically cognitive-behavioural techniques for balanced mental, emotional, and spiritual health.	The integration of *salāh* with conventional therapy helped Sarah find peace, meaning, and resilience in her life.

calm and Divine connection. Carter (2006) also noted that if clients wish to include prayer with their therapist, this should be welcomed respectfully, as it can enhance healing and therapeutic rapport. Acknowledging such practices not only fosters trust but also creates a holistic space for healing, addressing both psychological and spiritual well-being. Table 8.8 outlines the core elements of Sarah's case.

Sadaqah (charity)

Sadaqah, or voluntary charity, extends beyond financial giving; it embodies generosity, compassion, and selflessness. In therapy, it can support clients facing depression, isolation, or purposelessness by shifting their focus from internal struggles to helping others. Acts of charity foster emotional well-being, purpose, and community connection, reducing feelings of despair and selfishness.

Take the case of Mr. Ahmed, a 45-year-old man dealing with chronic depression, hopelessness, and social withdrawal. Despite therapy and medication, he struggled to find meaning or joy. His therapist, alongside using Islāmically integrated CBT (I-CBT), introduced *sadaqah* as a therapeutic tool. The suggestion included small, regular donations or simple acts of kindness like volunteering. Initially resistant, Mr. Ahmed felt too burdened to help others. However, the therapist explained that giving could break self-focused thought patterns and nurture gratitude. He was especially encouraged to support orphans, inspired by a hadīth in which the Prophet Muhammad (ﷺ) said: "The one who cares for an orphan – whether related or not, will be with me in Paradise like this," and he joined his index and middle fingers (Muslim). This guidance helped Mr. Ahmed connect his struggles with the suffering of others, sparking empathy and restoring a sense of purpose through compassionate action. Over time, as Mr. Ahmed began giving *sadaqah*, donating to orphanages and volunteering at local community centres, his feelings of isolation lessened, and he felt more connected to those around him. His depressive symptoms gradually subsided, and he began to experience moments of peace and fulfillment. The integration of charitable acts with psychosocial approaches like I-CBT helped him rediscover purpose and joy. This holistic approach led to a significant emotional and psychological shift, easing his depression and strengthening his sense of community and spiritual connection. Table 8.9 summarises Mr. Ahmed's therapeutic case.

Ruqyah (incantations)

Ruqyah is an Islāmic spiritual healing practice that involves reciting specific Qur'ānic verses and prophetic supplications (*du'ā'h*) for protection and healing. It is commonly used in cases where individuals believe they are affected

Table 8.9 Summarising the case vignette of Mr. Ahmed

Client details	Therapeutic interventions	Outcomes
45-year-old man, Mr. Ahmed struggled with chronic depression, hopelessness, and isolation. Limited response to medication and therapy alone	Islāmic Cognitive Behavioural Therapy (I-CBT) to address negative thought patterns Behavioural activation Introduction of *sadaqah* (charity) Islāmic Integrated Narrative Therapy (IINT)	Improved mood and decreased depressive symptoms Renewed sense of purpose and community connection Emotional and spiritual healing through giving
Background in Islāmic faith Disconnected from community and lacking daily motivation	Encouraged to perform small acts of kindness and financial donations Focus on caring for orphans (based on prophetic Hadith) Volunteer involvement	Reported increased joy from helping others Shifted focus from internal struggles to external contribution Greater life satisfaction
Initially resistant to charity Doubted its effect on mental health	Therapist reframed Sadaqah as a psychosocial and spiritual tool Connected religious practice with therapeutic goals	Built empathy and gratitude Felt spiritually uplifted and less burdened by depression Developed consistent engagement in charitable activities

by spiritual ailments such as the evil eye (*ayn*), jinn possession, or black magic (*siḥr*). In therapeutic settings, *ruqyah* can be a valuable psychospiritual intervention, particularly for clients who attribute their psychological distress to supernatural causes. For Muslim clients presenting with symptoms like unexplained physical pain, intrusive thoughts, hallucinations, or intense anxiety, especially when tied to religious or cultural beliefs, *ruqyah* may provide both spiritual comfort and psychological reassurance. Incorporating *ruqyah* can also help bridge the gap between religious healing practices and psychological therapy, affirming the client's worldview and strengthening the therapeutic alliance. While some qualified Islāmic psychotherapists may be able to incorporate elements of ruqyah within therapy, it is typically recommended to refer clients to a trained *rāqī*, a practitioner well-versed in the Qur'ān and prophetic traditions who follows authentic Islāmic guidelines. When used ethically and in collaboration with other professionals, *ruqyah* can become part of a holistic care plan. It supports spiritual validation, enhances the client's sense of agency, and provides relief, particularly in cases where standard treatments may not fully address culturally or spiritually rooted concerns. For a comprehensive literature on *ruqyah* and spiritual interventions see (Latif et al., 2014; Rassool, 2019).

References

An-Nasa'i. *Sunan an-Nasa'i 1168*.In-book reference: Book 12, Hadith 140. English translation: Vol. 2, Book 12, Hadith 1169. Sahih (Darussalam). https://sunnah.com/ nasai:1168

Carter, D. J. (2006). Spiritual/transactional integration with Asian/Islāmic clients. In S. D. Ambrose (Ed.), *Religion and psychology: New research* (pp. 241–255). Nova Science Publisher.

Islāmqa (2024). *Virtues of Dhikr*. https://islamqa.info/en/answers/253005/virtues-of-dhikr

Latif, J., Dockrat, S., & Rassool, G. Hussein. (2024). *Integrating spiritual interventions in Islāmic psychology a practical guide*. Focus Series on Islāmic Psychology & Psychotherapy. Routledge.

Muslim. *Sahih Muslim 2983*. In-book reference: Book 55, Hadith 52.USC-MSA web (English) reference: Book 42, Hadith 7108. https://sunnah.com/muslim:2983.

Rassool, G. Hussein. (2019). *Evil eye, Jinn possession, and mental health issues: An Islāmic perspective*. Routledge.

Tan, S. Y. (1996). Religion in clinical practice: Implicit and explicit integration. In E. Shafranske (Ed.), *Religion and the clinical practice of psychology* (pp. 365–390). American Psychological Association.

Tirmidhî (a). *Jami` at-Tirmidhî 3119*. In-book reference: Book 47, Hadith 171. English translation: Vol. 5, Book 44, Hadith 311. Sahih (Darussalam). https://sunnah.com/ tirmidhi:3119.

9 Clinical applications

Qur'ânic stories and metaphors

Storytelling from the Prophets: clinical applications

The narratives of Prophets Yusuf (عليهم السلام), Musa (عليه السلام), Ayyub (السلام عليه), and Yunus (عليه السلام) provide deeply therapeutic models that resonate with a wide range of emotional and psychological struggles in clinical settings.

The story of Prophet Yusuf (عليهم السلام) is profoundly resonant for clients who have endured deep interpersonal trauma, especially within the family unit, betrayals by those closest to them, experiences of being falsely accused or misunderstood, or enduring periods of extreme isolation and loss of control. His journey from the depths of a well to the darkness of a prison, and ultimately to a position of dignity and leadership, offers a powerful framework for understanding trauma, injustice, and the path to healing. Prophet Yusuf's (عليهم السلام) ability to maintain integrity, remain spiritually connected, and ultimately forgive those who wronged him serves as a rich therapeutic resource. His story can help clients reframe their suffering not as a sign of divine neglect, but as part of a greater unfolding wisdom, where adversity can be a means of purification, growth, and elevation.

The following vignette illustrates how the story of Prophet Yusuf (السلام عليهم) can be used in clinical therapy to help clients reframe their suffering, recognise the potential for spiritual growth, and ultimately find empowerment and healing. Fatima, a 28-year-old schoolteacher, enters therapy following years of estrangement from her family. As a teenager, she disclosed sexual abuse by a relative, an act that led to her being blamed, ostracised, and labelled a troublemaker. Her siblings sided with the abuser, accusing her of dishonouring the family. As a result, Fatima now experiences intense feelings of abandonment, mistrust, and emotional numbness. She struggles with depression and heightened sensitivity in relationships, feeling "trapped" by her past. In therapy, Fatima is introduced to the story of Prophet Yusuf (عليهم السلام), who was betrayed by his brothers, cast into a well, sold into slavery, and later imprisoned for a crime he was not responsible. Despite all this, Prophet Yusuf (عليهم السلام)

DOI: 10.4324/9781003584995-11

remained steadfast and did not allow his suffering to define his character or faith. When he was later reunited with his brothers, he chose forgiveness over revenge, saying:

قَالَ لَا تَثْرِيبَ عَلَيْكُمُ ٱلْيَوْمَ يَغْفِرُ ٱللَّهُ لَكُمْ وَهُوَ أَرْحَمُ ٱلرَّٰحِمِينَ

- *No blame will there be upon you today. Allāh will forgive you; and He is the most merciful of the merciful.*(Yusuf 12:92, interpretation of the meaning)

Fatima's therapeutic journey illustrates how sacred storytelling – particularly the narrative of Prophet Yusuf (عليهم السلام) can serve as a powerful tool for trauma recovery and identity reconstruction. This sacred narrative opens space for Fatima to reflect on her own journey, not to minimise the pain she has experienced, but to begin reframing it. She is supported in acknowledging her rightful anger and grief, while also recognising that forgiveness can be an act of liberation rather than submission. Through trauma-informed support, her emotions of anger, grief, and betrayal were validated without pressure, allowing her to safely process her pain and begin the slow journey towards healing. The parallel between her life and Yusuf's story enabled a form of symbolic co-regulation, offering emotional distance while still engaging with the core of her experiences. As the therapy progressed, spiritual integration became central to Fatima's healing. Reflecting on Prophet Yusuf's (عليهم السلام) patience and divine trust allowed her to view her suffering not as a punishment or abandonment, but as part of a larger, sacred journey. Forgiveness was reimagined as a spiritual liberation, freeing her from the emotional weight of resentment. She gained the strength to set healthy boundaries and prioritise her self-worth independently of her family's approval. Hope therapy (Rassool, 2025) within Fatima's therapeutic process centres on cultivating a sense of optimism rooted in spiritual trust. The therapist helps her reframe her hardships not as the end of her story, but as part of a meaningful, divinely guided journey. Drawing upon the prophetic model, particularly Prophet Yusuf's (عليهم السلام) endurance and eventual triumph, Fatima begins to internalise the belief that healing and justice are possible, even after deep suffering. Over time, hope becomes a sustaining force, guiding her towards long-term psychological and spiritual growth. She starts to reconnect with her spiritual identity, gradually loosens the grip of resentment, and sets healthy boundaries with her family. Ultimately, Fatima's growth was marked by a profound shift in self-perception, from someone broken by betrayal to a resilient woman deeply rooted in faith, meaning, and purpose. Table 9.1 presents the therapeutic takeaways, process, and outcome from Fatima's case.

Prophet Musa's (عليهم السلام) early life trauma, being separated from his mother, raised in a palace of oppression, and burdened with the responsibility of leadership, makes his story especially relevant for clients facing anxiety, imposter syndrome, or developmental trauma. In the case of Ahmed, a

Table 9.1 Therapeutic takeaways, process, and outcome from Fatima's case

Therapeutic theme	Application/ intervention	Client experience	Outcome
Narrative reframing	Paralleling Fatima's story with that of Prophet Yusuf (عليهم السلام).	Begins to see forgiveness as reclaiming her story, not submission.	Reclaims sense of control and redefines her identity beyond trauma.
Trauma-informed support	Validating grief and anger in a safe therapeutic space.	Feels heard and understood; able to express suppressed emotions.	Emotional regulation and gradual healing.
Spiritual integration	Reflecting on the dignity, patience, and spiritual wisdom in Yusuf's journey.	Connects with divine wisdom behind suffering.	Reframes pain as part of a meaningful spiritual journey.
Forgiveness	Encouraged to journal and reflect on forgiveness from a position of strength.	Views forgiveness as freeing herself from resentment.	Moves from victimhood to emotional and spiritual freedom.
Hope therapy	Therapy nurtures optimism, trust in divine wisdom, and belief in future healing despite past harm.	Prophetic resilience in adversity; Allah's mercy and justice.	Strengthened hope, motivation to heal, and long-term psychological growth.
Empowerment & boundaries	Supporting healthy boundaries with family and affirming self-worth outside of their approval.	Feels stronger, more self-directed.	Establishes boundaries and strengthens self-worth rooted in faith.

19-year-old who fears public speaking due to childhood silencing, the story of Musa (عليهم السلام) becomes a powerful source of identification. By learning about Musa's own hesitation and the divine du'ā' he recited before speaking ("O my Lord, open for me my chest..." Taha 20:25–28), Ahmed begins to regulate his anxiety, developing confidence through spiritual practice and prophetic modelling.

Prophet Ayyub's (عليه السلام) life exemplifies unwavering faith amid immense suffering. His story is particularly meaningful for clients who feel trapped in chronic pain, long-term illness, or emotional despair. In therapy, his endurance is not interpreted as blind resignation but as conscious spiritual patience (*ṣabr*), grounded in a deep trust in Allāh's wisdom. For Saliha, a 42-year-old woman managing a debilitating illness, Ayyub's story helps her shift from a narrative of hopelessness to one of purposeful endurance. Rather than feeling spiritually punished, she begins to view her patience as an act of faith, allowing her to reconnect with her religious identity and find strength in small, consistent acts of resilience. The story helps reframe her suffering as part of a sacred process that can still yield restoration and healing.

Prophet Yunus (عليه السلام) represents the spiritual journey from despair and isolation to repentance and renewal. His time in the belly of the whale becomes a symbol of emotional and existential darkness, a place where many clients feel trapped when facing depression, burnout, or a sense of divine abandonment. Bilal, a 32-year-old man devastated by divorce and job loss, finds profound comfort in Yunus's plea from the depths: "There is no deity except You; exalted are You. Indeed, I have been of the wrongdoers" (Al-Anbiya 21:87). This verse, full of vulnerability and self-awareness, allows Bilal to process his guilt without shame and begin the journey towards spiritual and emotional healing. Reconnecting with faith helps him reclaim his sense of worth and reminds him that divine mercy is never out of reach.

Prophet Yusuf's (عليهم السلام), like those of Prophet Musa's (عليهم السلام) and Prophet Ayyub's (عليه السلام), highlight a therapeutic pathway where prophetic experience becomes a means for clients to access hope, reframe their pain, and begin meaningful inner transformation.

Metaphorical reframing through an Islāmic lens

In the realm of Islāmic Modified Narrative Therapy, metaphorical reframing takes on additional layers of meaning through its interconnection with the rich spiritual imagery and teachings of the Qur'ān and *Sunnah*. Rather than solely altering a client's cognitive framework, this method attaches their narrative within a context of divine wisdom and purposeful struggle. It invites clients to view their challenges as integral aspects of a broader spiritual journey, but as meaningful experiences laden with the potential to inspire hope, encourage personal responsibility, and deepen trust in Allāh's benevolent guidance. A practical example of this faith-based reframe can be observed in a scenario where a client articulates feelings of desolation. For example, consider a client who expresses deep feelings of desolation with the statement,

Client's statement: *I feel like I'm walking in darkness and I don't know where I'm going.*
This expression of existential uncertainty and disconnection from purpose is a common refrain in times of emotional despair. Within an Islāmic framework,

such a statement is not only acknowledged but is rein-
terpreted in light of divine promise and guidance. The
therapist might gently reframe the client's experience
by saying,

Therapist's reframe: *It sounds like you are in a place of darkness, but Allāh*
tells us in the Qur'ān that He brings the believer out
of darkness into light. Maybe you're not lost, maybe
you're in the process of being guided through a tunnel
into the light, and this phase is part of that journey.

The Qur'ānic verse is:

ٱللَّهُ وَلِيُّ ٱلَّذِينَ ءَامَنُوٱ يُخْرِجُهُم مِّنَ ٱلظُّلُمَٰتِ إِلَى ٱلنُّورِ ۖ

- *Allāh is the ally of those who believe. He brings them out from dark-
nesses into the light.* (Al-Baqarah 2:257, interpretation of the meaning)

This reframe is powerfully evocative for several reasons. First, it aligns
the client's personal experience with a well-established Qur'ānic teaching,
reminding them that they are not alone in their struggle. The imagery of
a tunnel leading into the light serves as a tangible metaphor for transition
and transformation, a passage through hardship towards eventual clarity
and renewal. In this light, the client's feelings of wandering in darkness are
reframed not as a permanent state, but as a temporary phase that has inherent
purpose and value. Such a perspective provides a dual benefit: it validates
the client's emotional experience while simultaneously pointing to a hopeful future where divine guidance will usher them into clarity and warmth.
Moreover, this approach enriches the therapeutic process by fostering a
deep sense of spiritual connection. By internalising this message, clients
can begin to see themselves as active participants in a larger narrative, one
that is dynamic and ultimately redemptive. This perspective can be especially transformative for clients who might otherwise feel overwhelmed by
their struggles, as it shifts the focus from existential despair to the promise
of future light and guidance.

Case vignette: Leyla and the invisible burden

The following case illustrates how a Qur'ānic metaphor, in this instance, the
concept of carrying a burden, can be used as a therapeutic entry point for
scrupulosity and anxiety.

Leyla, a 20-year-old university student, sought therapy after months of
debilitating anxiety, guilt, and confusion. A devout Muslim from a conservative
family, Leyla appeared bright, committed to her religious practice, and deeply
sincere in her faith. However, beneath this devotion lay a chronic and distressing condition: she was overwhelmed by obsessive religious thought (*waswas*),
what she described as *"dirty whispers about Allāh,"* feelings of perpetual guilt,

and the unbearable fear of being punished for thoughts she never intended to have. Leyla would perform wudu (ritual purification) repeatedly, sometimes up to ten times in a row, terrified that she had made a mistake. She prayed five times daily, but each *salah* took nearly an hour because of intrusive doubts about her recitation and intention. She feared even touching the Qur'ân without perfect ritual purity, and she avoided social settings, worried that laughter or idle talk would invalidate her faith. Despite knowing that Islām does not demand such extremes, Leyla felt trapped in an inner courtroom, constantly being judged by her own mind.

In one session, after Leyla broke down crying and said,

Leyla:	*"I feel like I'm carrying the weight of the world on my shoulders, and no one can help me unload it,"*
Therapist:	Introduced a Qur'ânic metaphor. Leyla, there is a verse in Surah Al-An'am that speaks directly to people who feel exactly as you do. It says, *"No bearer of burdens shall bear the burden of another."* What does that mean to you?
Leyla:	That... I don't have to carry everything alone?
Therapist:	*Not just that. It means you were never meant to. You are not responsible for intrusive thoughts you didn't invite. You're not accountable for what whispers come to your mind. Faith is not perfection; it is trust. And Allāh knows the difference between what you do and what you fear you've done.*
	Leyla sat silently for a moment, then nodded, tears in her eyes.
Leyla:	*But what if I accidentally think something wrong and don't realise it? What if I didn't say my intention right? What if... I'm not really a believer?*
Therapist:	*These are the burdens you have been trying to carry, but they were never yours to hold. What if your journey isn't about avoiding every mistake, but about trusting that Allāh is Merciful even when you fall?*
	We explored how her obsessive thoughts (*waswasa*) were not sins, but symptoms. Through structured Islāmically modified cognitive-behavioural therapy (I-CBT) tailored to religious scrupulosity, combined with spiritual reframing, gentle exposure, *ruqyah* and Islāmic teachings on mercy and ease, Leyla began to reclaim her peace. She started experimenting with trusting her first *wudu*. She allowed herself to pray without redoing every takbir. She even began to journal her thoughts, noting how often the burden she felt wasn't real – but perceived. Over several months,

Leyla developed a healthier relationship with her faith, recognising that what she thought was "piety" was, in fact, perfectionism driven by fear – not love or trust. She began to say things like:

Leyla: *I don't have to carry Allāh's judgment. That's not my burden. My job is to try... and then trust.*

This case exemplifies how a Qur'ânic metaphor, specifically, the idea of bearing a burden, can serve as a therapeutic gateway for addressing scrupulosity and anxiety. In Leyla's treatment, this metaphor was integrated with approaches such as I-CBT, self-compassion training, psychoeducation, *ruqyah* for *waswasa*, and gradual behavioural experiments. All of these techniques were contextualised within an Islāmic framework, ultimately working together to enhance both her spiritual and psychological well-being. Table 9.2 presents an outline of a clinical case study: Leyla and the invisible burden.

Application across client presentations

The Islāmic metaphors can be integrated with more general metaphorical reframing to address varied mental health challenges. For example, while a client with depression might be compared to a donkey carrying heavy books without truly engaging with their content (Al-Jumu'ah: 5), an Islāmic modified narrative lens could deepen that reframing by suggesting that the client, like one guided by divine wisdom, has the potential to transform routine obligations into steps towards spiritual enlightenment.

When working with a client who experiences depression, one useful metaphor is drawn from (Al-Jumu'ah 62:5):

كَمَثَلِ ٱلْحِمَارِ يَحْمِلُ أَسْفَارًا

- ... *Like that of a donkey who carries volumes [of books].* (Al-Jumu'ah 62:5, interpretation of the meaning).

The metaphor presents the client behaviour [not the client] as akin to a donkey burdened with heavy books, symbolising the weight of various obligations carried without true understanding. In this metaphor, the donkey represents an individual's behaviour who mechanically fulfills daily tasks without engaging with the deeper meaning behind them. The heavy books serve as a metaphor for the multiple responsibilities, including work, social duties, or personal commitments that are accumulated over time. However, these books, laden with content the donkey never truly comprehends, symbolise tasks and roles performed superficially, lacking genuine insight or emotional engagement.

Table 9.2 Clinical case study: Leyla and the invisible burden

Category	Details	Notes/insights
Presenting issue	Chronic anxiety, religious scrupulosity (*waswasa*), and obsessive-compulsive behaviours disrupting daily and spiritual life.	Leyla's condition aligns with Religious Obsessional Compulsive Disorder (OCD); spiritual distress was deeply linked to her psychological symptoms.
Background	Twenty-year-old devout Muslim raised in a conservative environment. Increasing rigidity and fear-based religious practices.	Rigid upbringing contributed to moral perfectionism and guilt.
Symptoms	Excessive *wudu* (up to ten times), prolonged prayer rituals, avoidance of social settings, and intrusive thoughts.	Religious rituals became compulsions; intrusive thoughts viewed as moral failings.
Therapeutic approach	Integration of I-CBT for OCD and Islāmic psychotherapy including Qur'ânic metaphor reframing.	Emphasised balance between spiritual devotion and psychological health.
Key metaphor	Qur'anic verse: "No bearer of burdens shall bear the burden of another" (Surah Al-An'am: 164, interpretation of the meaning).	Helped Leyla separate symptoms from sin and moral judgement; led to self-compassion.
Dialogue highlight Leyla: *That I don't have to carry everything alone?*	Therapist: *What does this verse mean to you?* Therapist: *Exactly, you were never meant to.*	This moment was pivotal; the metaphor created emotional clarity and opened space for change
Interventions used	Cognitive restructuring ERP for ritual behaviours Journaling and self-reflection Islāmic psychoeducation (mercy, waswasa, spiritual ease).	All interventions were framed within Leyla's worldview, improving engagement and outcomes.
Outcomes	Leyla gained insight, reduced compulsions, improved functionality, and restored trust in her spiritual path.	Leyla's reflection: "*My job is to try... and then trust.*"
Conclusion	Metaphoric therapy grounded in Islāmic texts empowered Leyla to overcome internalised guilt and obsessive behaviours.	Demonstrates value of combining faith-sensitive therapy with evidence-based practices.

This metaphor draws attention to how individuals might navigate their everyday life, moving through routines that are routine and obligatory, rather than inspired by personal connection or purpose. The behaviour of the individual becomes mere repetition, devoid of the meaningful involvement that could otherwise enrich one's experiences. Within a therapeutic context, this imagery serves as a powerful tool for discussion, inviting clients to examine whether their routines are acted out as habit or filled with personal significance. Therapists can use this metaphor to ask insightful questions, such as whether the client feels their daily activities are simply tasks to be performed, or if they resonate on a deeper emotional level. By reinterpreting their responsibilities through this metaphor, clients may start to realise that there exists an opportunity to transform routine behaviour into a pathway for deeper personal meaning. In essence, the imagery of the donkey carrying heavy books without understanding their contents provides a vivid and relatable metaphor that can help clients explore and redefine their experiences, paving the way for a more enriched and meaningful engagement with life.

For clients struggling with anxiety, the metaphor from (Al-Ankabut: 41) provides a vivid illustration.

مَثَلُ ٱلَّذِينَ ٱتَّخَذُواْ مِن دُونِ ٱللَّهِ أَوْلِيَآءَ كَمَثَلِ ٱلْعَنكَبُوتِ ٱتَّخَذَتْ بَيْتًا ۖ وَإِنَّ أَوْهَنَ ٱلْبُيُوتِ لَبَيْتُ ٱلْعَنكَبُوتِ ۖ لَوْ كَانُواْ يَعْلَمُونَ

- *The example of those who take allies other than Allāh is like that of the spider who takes a home. And indeed, the weakest of homes is the home of the spider – if they only knew.* (Al-'Ankabūt 29: 41, interpretation of the meaning)

Much like a spider weaves a delicate web in the hope of creating a safe and secure space, individuals struggling with anxiety often construct intricate mental frameworks based on constant worry and hypothetical "*what if*" scenarios. These mental constructs, although designed to offer a sense of protection or control, are often as fragile as the spider's web, which is easily disrupted when exposed to real-life pressures. Just as the spider's web cannot withstand harsh winds or sudden force, these cognitive patterns collapse when tested against the unpredictability of life, leaving the individual feeling even more vulnerable and overwhelmed. This metaphor can be a powerful therapeutic tool, helping clients visualise how their anxious thinking may be giving the illusion of safety while actually reinforcing their fears. By drawing on this metaphor, therapists can gently challenge clients to explore the effectiveness of their anxiety-driven thought processes. Clients can be invited to examine whether their habitual overthinking and repetitive self-questioning are truly protective, or if these strategies are inadvertently increasing their mental burden. Therapists might ask,

- *Is this thought helping you or weighing you down,* or
- *Is the structure you've built in your mind a source of comfort, or a trap of your own making?*

In doing so, clients are encouraged to step back and reflect on the functionality of their internal coping mechanisms. This shift in perspective opens the door to developing more grounded and flexible coping strategies, ones that promote genuine resilience rather than reinforcing the illusion of safety through anxious rumination.

In clinical practice, the metaphors from An-Nahl 16:25 and An-Najm 53:38 can be powerful tools for helping a client with low self-esteem develop a deeper understanding of their personal responsibility, the impact of their actions, and the importance of reclaiming their sense of self-worth:

لِيَحْمِلُوٓا۟ أَوْزَارَهُمْ كَامِلَةً يَوْمَ ٱلْقِيَـٰمَةِ ۙ وَمِنْ أَوْزَارِ ٱلَّذِينَ يُضِلُّونَهُم بِغَيْرِ عِلْمٍ ۗ أَلَا سَآءَ مَا يَزِرُونَ

- *And they will bear their own burdens in full on the Day of Judgment, along with some of the burdens of those whom they misled without knowledge. Woe to them for what they bear.* (An-Nahl 16:25, interpretation of the meaning)

In therapy, this verse can be applied to help a client reflect on the weight of unnecessary emotional burdens they may carry, burdens that often come from external pressures or the expectations of others. For a client with low self-esteem, these "burdens" might manifest as feelings of inadequacy, fear of judgement, or guilt for perceived failures. A therapeutic approach might involve helping the client understand that while they may feel responsible for others' emotions or reactions, they are not accountable for others' perceptions or actions. It is important to help the client distinguish between what they can control, their own actions and though, and what they cannot, which is the way others may respond or the judgements they impose. This reflection on personal responsibility can help alleviate the pressure they feel in trying to meet the expectations of others. For example, a therapist might ask,

- *Do you sometimes feel responsible for how others perceive you or react to you?*
- *How does that impact how you view yourself?*

This can open the door to exploring how the client's self-worth may be tied to the approval or validation of others, and how releasing that unnecessary burden can help them begin to cultivate healthier self-esteem.

Similarly, in An-Najm 53:38. Allāh says:

أَلَّا تَزِرُ وَازِرَةٌ وِزْرَ أُخْرَىٰ

- *That no bearer of burdens will bear the burden of another.* (An-Najm 53:38 interpretation of the meaning)

This verse reinforces the concept of individual responsibility, helping clients understand that they are not responsible for carrying the emotional weight of others, nor are they required to live up to others' unrealistic expectations. For a client with low self-esteem, this can be a crucial reminder to take ownership of their own life and actions, while letting go of the belief that they are burdened by the expectations, mistakes, or needs of others. Therapists can use this verse to help the client explore how they may be carrying unnecessary emotional baggage, such as the guilt of not meeting others' standards, and gently guide them towards releasing those burdens. For example, a therapist might say

- *It sounds like you're shouldering a lot of expectations from others, but remember that you are not responsible for their happiness or actions.*
- *How can we begin to shift the focus back to what you need in order to feel whole and authentic?*

This approach encourages the client to take ownership of their own emotions and self-worth, instead of allowing external validation to determine their value. By fostering an understanding of the balance between personal accountability and releasing unnecessary burdens, clients can develop a healthier sense of self-esteem that comes from within, rather than relying on external approval. In summary, these verses can be used as a way to help clients with low self-esteem recognise the importance of distinguishing between their own responsibilities and those of others. Encouraging clients to reflect on how they might be carrying emotional burdens unnecessarily, while also empowering them to recognise their intrinsic worth and personal accountability, can lead to a more resilient and authentic sense of self.

For those dealing with the lasting impact of trauma, the metaphor from At-Taubah 9: 109 can be instructive:

أَفَمَنْ أَسَّسَ بُنْيَٰنَهُ عَلَىٰ تَقْوَىٰ مِنَ ٱللَّهِ وَرِضْوَٰنٍ خَيْرٌ أَم مَّنْ أَسَّسَ بُنْيَٰنَهُ عَلَىٰ
شَفَا جُرُفٍ هَارٍ فَٱنْهَارَ بِهِۦ فِى نَارِ جَهَنَّمَۗ وَٱللَّهُ لَا يَهْدِى ٱلْقَوْمَ ٱلظَّٰلِمِينَ

- *Then is one who laid the foundation of his building on righteousness [with fear] from Allāh and [seeking] His approval better, or one who laid the foundation of his building on the edge of a bank about to collapse, so it collapsed with him into the Fire of Hell? And Allāh does not guide the wrongdoing people.* (At-Tawbah 9:109, interpretation of the meaning)

The verse draws a powerful comparison between two types of foundations: one built upon righteousness, fear of Allāh, and His approval, and another built upon a crumbling, unstable edge that leads to collapse and destruction. This metaphor can be deeply meaningful when working with clients who struggle with low self-esteem, as it invites reflection on the foundations upon which they have built their sense of self-worth. In therapeutic work, this verse can help the client explore whether their self-concept is rooted in solid, intrinsic values, such as sincerity, personal growth, spiritual awareness, and a connection to Allāh, or if it is based on fragile and unstable sources, like the need for external validation, comparisons, social approval, or perfectionism. When a person builds their identity on what others think, on fleeting standards of success, or on unresolved shame, it becomes like building on the edge of a crumbling bank: it cannot withstand the trials of life and inevitably leads to internal collapse, manifesting as anxiety, depression, or deep insecurity. Encouraging the client to *"rebuild their internal foundation"* with sincerity (*ikhlas*), *taqwa* (consciousness of Allāh), and a commitment to what pleases Allāh , not what pleases people, can be transformative. The verse reminds us that true stability comes from aligning one's life with divine values, not from chasing unstable worldly affirmations. By internalising this message, the client can begin to shift from a shaky self-image to a grounded sense of self that is less vulnerable to criticism and rejection and more connected to their spiritual and moral core.

This process might include:

• Exploring what values the client wants to live by.
• Identifying thoughts and behaviours that reflect the *"a bank about to collapse."*
• Supporting them to define success and worth in terms of their relationship with Allāh and inner growth.

This Qur'ânic metaphor can thus be a powerful therapeutic tool to help clients reframe their narrative, find spiritual resilience, and reconstruct their self-esteem on firm, unshakeable ground.

Finally, for clients struggling with addictive behaviours, the Qur'ân ic metaphor from An-Noor 24:3: offers a meaningful perspective.

> ▪ *Allāh is the Light of the heavens and the earth. The example of His light is like a niche within which is a lamp, the lamp is within glass, the glass as if it were a pearly [white] star lit from [the oil of] a blessed olive tree, neither of the east nor of the west, whose oil would almost glow even if untouched by fire. Light upon light. Allāh guides to His light whom He wills. And Allāh presents examples for the people, and Allāh is Knowing of all things.* (An-Noor 24:35, interpretation of the meaning)

These verses evoke the image of an inner light hidden beneath layers of burdens, symbolising how addictive patterns can obscure a person's inherent brilliance. Addiction often thrives in isolation, secrecy, guilt, shame, and emotional pain. Clients may feel spiritually disconnected, broken, or unworthy of healing. By reflecting on how these behaviours might be covering up their true potential, therapists can help clients identify and work through the underlying issues, be they emotional pain, unmet needs, or unresolved conflicts, that sustain their addiction, ultimately encouraging a pathway towards recovery and self-illumination. This verse also presents a hope-filled metaphor: no matter how lost someone feels, there is a niche within the heart, an inner space, where Allāh's light can still reside. In clinical settings, the metaphor can be used to challenge shame-based narratives. Clients may believe they are beyond redemption or inherently flawed. The metaphor of a *lamp within a glass* can help reframe this by showing that beneath the layers of self-destruction is a pure light that still exists and can be rekindled.

Therapist prompt:

- *What would it mean to you if there is still a source of light inside, even if you can't see it right now?*

The image of the lamp glowing even before being touched by fire suggests that the potential for recovery is already present, waiting to be activated. It emphasises that change does not start from outside, it begins with recognising one's inner strength and divine connection.

The therapeutic focus is to support the client in identifying moments of clarity, conscience, or spiritual yearning, even in the midst of addiction. This verse allows therapists to anchor discussions around purpose, identity, and divine guidance, helping clients realign their behaviours with their deeper values. A reflective question would be.

- *What would your life look like if you allowed that light to guide your actions again?*

By using this Qur'ânic metaphor thoughtfully in therapy, practitioners can offer clients a non-judgemental, compassionate space to reflect, reframe their identity, and build a bridge from suffering to spiritual healing, all while reinforcing the belief in the client's innate capacity for transformation. Each of these metaphors, while rooted in Islāmic tradition, also carries a universal appeal that extends to the secular understanding of our shared human struggles. Using such imagery provides clients with a rich, symbolic language to articulate their inner experiences, fostering both insight and transformative growth in the therapeutic process. Table 9.3 provides an outline of the clinical application of Qur'ânic metaphors across client presentations.

Table 9.3 Application of Qur'ānic metaphor across client presentations

Client presentation	Metaphorical reframing (Qur'ânic imagery)	Therapeutic application
Depression	Al-Jumu'ah 62:5: Like a donkey carrying books without understanding their meaning (interpretation of the meaning).	Explore emotional disconnection: Ask if daily routines feel like mere obligations without genuine engagement.
Anxiety	Al-'Ankabūt 29: 41. Like a spider building a fragile web for protection that ultimately crumbles under heavy doubt meaning (interpretation of the meaning).	Challenge excessive worry: Invite reflection on whether relentless "what ifs" truly provide security or only add burden.

(Continued)

Table 9.3 Continued

Client presentation	Metaphorical reframing (Qur'ānic imagery)	Therapeutic application
Low self-esteem	An-Nahl 16:25 and An-Najm 53:38: success may not illuminate one's inner self (interpretation of the meaning).	Encourage self-reflection: Ask if meeting external expectations truly validates personal worth or if intrinsic value is missing.
Trauma	At-Tawbah: 9:109, Repeating unresolved burdens, like carrying weight repeatedly without processing it (interpretation of the meaning).	Foster trauma processing: Discuss what it might look like to set down the repeated burden and explore healing steps.
Addictive behaviours	An-Noor 24:35. An inner light obscured by layers of burdens, blocking authentic self-expression (interpretation of the meaning).	Enhance self-awareness: Reflect on how habits mask inner strengths and discuss ways to uncover one's true potential.

Reference

Rassool, G. Hussein. (2025). *Islāmic counselling & psychotherapy* (2nd ed.). Routledge.

10 Challenges and considerations

Reflections

The Islāmically Integrated Narrative Therapy (IINT) model is a therapeutic framework designed to blend the principles of narrative therapy with the rich spiritual and theological heritage of Islām. At the core of the model lies the Islāmic theological foundation: the Oneness of God (*Tawḥīd*), reliance on Him (*tawakkul*), and belief in divine decree (*qadar*). This provides clients with a stable spiritual anchor, helping them interpret their life events through a lens of divine wisdom and purpose. By acknowledging that all experiences, struggles, and successes are part of the divine plan, the therapist and client can engage in a transformative process that connects personal narratives with a broader, divinely guided purpose. The component of the client's narrative centres the client's voice and lived experience. It encourages clients to share their personal stories, explore their identity, and articulate how they perceive their life events. This self-reflection is the first step towards transformation. With therapeutic guidance, clients are supported in reinterpreting their past experiences.

Islāmic teachings and metaphors assist in reshaping narratives of pain, loss, or injustice into stories of endurance, faith, and growth. The spiritual interventions include practices such as *dhikr* (remembrance of Allāh), *du'āh* (supplication), recitation of Qur'ânic verses, and reflection on the names and attributes of Allāh. Such interventions nurture spiritual connection and emotional regulation. Drawing from the stories of Prophets (عليه السلام), clients find relatable and inspiring narratives that parallel their own struggles. Through the therapeutic use of these stories, clients are not only reminded of the virtues of perseverance and hope but also see themselves as part of a larger, divinely orchestrated narrative that ultimately leads to healing and growth. Islāmic metaphors, such as life as a test, the heart as a vessel, or light vs. darknes, serve as therapeutic tools. They enable indirect engagement with trauma, facilitating insight without triggering emotional overwhelm. Islāmic healing is not just individual but communal. This component emphasises the importance of social support, shared values, and collective accountability in

DOI: 10.4324/9781003584995-12

recovery and reintegration. Clients are encouraged to become active participants in their healing journey, taking ownership of their stories while integrating Islāmic values into their narratives. The process is about empowering
them to find their own spiritual path within their personal narrative. This
empowerment is central to the IINT's model, which fosters a sense of ownership over one's life story and emotional healing.

The integrative nature of the IINT model ensures that clients are not
viewed solely through the prism of psychological symptoms, but as complete human beings encompassing emotional, mental, and spiritual dimensions. This holistic framework invites clients to delve into their inner worlds
while fostering a meaningful relationship with Allāh. Through this process,
healing emerges at the intersection of faith, personal narrative, and divine
wisdom. As clients reflect on their life stories, they are guided to reinterpret
their experiences as opportunities for self-awareness, spiritual elevation,
and inner tranquility. IINT empowers individuals to find meaning in their
struggles by helping them construct narratives rooted in resilience, purpose,
and divine connection. It integrates the core techniques of narrative therapy
with Islāmic teachings, offering clients a spiritually grounded means of processing and reframing life events. In doing so, the model not only facili-
tates emotional healing but also nurtures the soul, helping clients develop
a deeper sense of tawakkul (trust in Allāh), gratitude, and hope. More than
a clinical method, IINT serves as a spiritually transformative journey. It
supports clients in aligning their healing with the wisdom of Islāmic tradition and their personal relationship with Allāh. In this sacred space, therapy
becomes an act of worship, reflection, and restoration, a path towards holistic well-being inspired by divine mercy and truth.

The IINT model places strong emphasis on the role of the therapist as
a compassionate and spiritually attuned guide. Unlike conventional therapeutic models that focus solely on psychological expertise, IINT calls for
practitioners who are well-versed in both psychological sciences and Islāmic
knowledge. This dual competency ensures that the therapeutic alliance is
not only clinically sound but also spiritually meaningful. The therapist, in
this framework, is not merely a facilitator of cognitive or emotional change
but a witness to the client's spiritual journey, offering guidance that aligns
with Islāmic values and principles. An IINT-trained therapist understands the
profound influence of faith on the client's worldview and is sensitive to the
sacred meanings clients attach to their struggles and healing processes. This
spiritual literacy allows the therapist to honour and integrate concepts such as
tawakkul (trust in God), *sabr* (patience), and *qadar* (divine decree), into the
narrative therapy process. These concepts are not used dogmatically but are
gently woven into the client's evolving story, empowering them to reframe
adversity in light of divine wisdom rather than random misfortune. Such spiritual alignment strengthens the client's sense of coherence, hope, and resilience. Moreover, therapists working within the IINT model strive to uphold a

therapeutic presence that is rooted in *adab* (etiquette), empathy, and humility. This creates a sacred therapeutic space where the client feels seen, heard, and spiritually supported. The therapist in the IINT model becomes a companion, someone who walks alongside the client in their pursuit of healing, growth, and spiritual integration. Their role is to create space for deep reflection, compassionate inquiry, and narrative reconstruction infused with divine meaning. This therapeutic relationship, grounded in both professional competence and spiritual integrity, becomes a powerful medium for holistic transformation.

When integrating Islāmic stories and principles into therapeutic practice, it is essential to acknowledge and to map a range of challenges and considerations that can arise.

Diversity in religiosity and spiritual orientation

A key challenge in integrating Islāmic content into therapy lies in the diversity of religiosity and their individual relationships with Islām among Muslim clients. While many adhere closely to Islāmic teachings, others identify primarily as cultural Muslims, engaging more with cultural traditions that do not always align with foundational Islāmic principles (Rassool, 2019). Muslim communities around the world are richly diverse, shaped by various cultural contexts despite a shared foundation of core religious values and practices. For instance, a client who regards their Muslim identity as part of their cultural background may find explicit religious references in therapy less meaningful or relevant. In such cases, applying a uniform religious lens may unintentionally create distance or reduce therapeutic effectiveness. Therapists must therefore remain attuned to each client's individual religious or cultural orientation in order to create a respectful, inclusive, and supportive therapeutic environment. For some, Qur'ānic reflections may offer clarity and solace; for others, metaphorical or secular interpretations may feel safer and more empowering. The therapist's task is to co-create a space where each client feels respected and in control of their narrative, allowing for an adaptive integration of faith that aligns with the client's personal worldview.

Respecting theological and cultural pluralism

Islām is practiced by a vast, culturally diverse global community. Clients come from various madhāb (legal schools), sects, and cultural traditions. What is spiritually meaningful for one individual may be unfamiliar or discomforting for another. Thus, the therapist must avoid assumptions about what "Islāmic" means for each client, and instead remain curious and open to each person's unique relationship with their faith. Therapists must be equipped to differentiate between what is culturally inherited and what is religiously grounded, especially when cultural norms contribute to the client's distress. For instance, rigid family expectations or gender roles may be presented as religious obligations when they are, in fact, cultural constructs. Therapists must be capable of differentiating between cultural constructs and authentic Islāmicteachings, helping clients explore religious meanings while gently challenging potentially harmful assumptions presented as religious truths.

Religious literacy and ethical integration

For IINT to be effective and respectful, religious literacy is essential on the part of the therapist. Practitioners must possess a grounded understanding of Islāmic studies and ethical frameworks to ensure the therapy remains theologically sound. This is particularly important when interpreting Qur'ānic verses or *hadīth* in a clinical context. Misrepresentation can not only damage the therapeutic alliance but also distort religious understanding. Clients too will vary in their knowledge and engagement with Islāmic concepts. Some may be well-versed in spiritual teachings, while others may be disconnected due to previous negative experiences with religious institutions. Imposing faith-based interpretations in such contexts risks invalidating the client's experience and undermining narrative therapy's client-centred ethos.

This presents a core challenge in integrating narrative therapy, which is inherently client-centred and places great emphasis on the individual's ability to author their own story. Balancing this principle with the presence of religious guidance from the Islāmic tradition requires careful and sensitive navigation.

Flexibility in application

Flexibility is central to IINT's success. Therapists must remain attuned to verbal and non-verbal cues, knowing when to pause, redirect, or adapt their approach. Hybrid models that incorporate trauma-informed care, cognitive therapy, and Islāmic principles are often most effective. For example, a client resonating with Prophet Yūnus's (عليه السلام) journey – from despair to renewal – might benefit from integrating Qur'ānic reflection with cognitive restructuring to challenge depressive thoughts. Similarly, a client processing betrayal may find strength in the story of Prophet Yūsuf (عليه السلام) but still require somatic-based interventions to process trauma physically. The therapist's role is to tailor interventions that honour both the client's psychological needs and spiritual language. This approach promotes not only emotional healing but also inner tranquility and deeper *tawakkul* (trust in Allāh).

The therapist as a spiritually attuned companion

In IINT, the therapist serves not merely as a facilitator of emotional change but as a compassionate, spiritually informed guide. Unlike conventional therapy models that emphasise clinical detachment, IINT emphasises relational depth rooted in *adab* (Islāmic etiquette), empathy, compassion, and humility. The therapist becomes a witness to the client's spiritual journey and helps them reframe adversity in light of divine wisdom rather than random misfortune. An IINT-trained therapist synthesises Islāmic principles, such as *sabr* (patience), *tawakkul* (trust), and *qadar* (divine decree), into the therapeutic process without coercion. These concepts are not imposed, but gently explored as part of the client's evolving story, empowering them to find coherence and meaning in their suffering. This alignment with faith supports a transformative healing process that restores not only psychological balance but also spiritual well-being.

Ongoing development and interdisciplinary collaboration

Given that IINT is a developing approach, therapists must commit to lifelong learning and reflective practice. This includes formal study of Islāmic psychology, consultation with scholars, and active participation in culturally competent supervision. Therapists must also explore their own assumptions and biases regarding Islām, particularly when integrating theological content into therapy. For non-Muslim practitioners, ethical IINT practice may require cultural consultation or co-facilitation with Muslim professionals. Such collaboration ensures greater sensitivity and theological accuracy while respecting the client's religious and cultural framework. As the field grows, continued dialogue between scholars, clinicians, and researchers will be key to refining the approach and building an evidence-informed, spiritually congruent therapeutic model.

Conclusion

IINT is not a one-size-fits-all method but a flexible, client-centred model that honours both the emotional complexity and spiritual richness of each individual. It holds significant promise as a modality for transformative healing, particularly for clients who seek a faith-informed approach to mental health. When practiced with humility, cultural sensitivity, and theological integrity, IINT empowers clients to reconnect with their values, draw strength from sacred narratives, and reclaim authorship over their life stories. By drawing on Qur'ânic stories, Prophetic experiences, and Islāmic metaphors, such as the transformation from darkness to light (*min al-ẓulumāt ila al-nūr*, therapists can help clients re-author their narratives in ways that restore agency, meaning, and hope. This approach empowers clients to reinterpret hardship through a redemptive lens, cultivating resilience and a deeper connection to their Creator. For therapists, the Islāmic tradition provides a rich, ethically grounded reservoir of symbols, parables, and teachings that can be employed meaningfully in therapy, making the process both clinically effective and spiritually uplifting. In doing so, therapy becomes more than clinical intervention, it becomes a sacred encounter, a path towards healing, meaning, and divine connection.

Reference

Rassool, G. Hussein. (2019). *Evil eye, Jinn possession, and mental health issues: The Islāmic perspective*. Routledge.

Index

For Product Safety Concerns and Information please contact our EU
representative GPSR@taylorandfrancis.com
Taylor & Francis Verlag GmbH, Kaufingerstraße 24, 80331 München, Germany